Seek. Find. Be.

Know Thyself as Conscious Creator

Kea Rivers

KNOW THYSELF SERIES – BOOK THREE

MIRROR LEAF
PRESS

ISBN: 9781969507038

First Edition

Printed in the United States of America

For permissions or inquiries, contact: riverskea@gmail.com

Contents

A Visual Key to the Journey...v
Symbolic Map of the Journey...ix
The Arc of Seek. Find. Be. xi
Preface...xiii

PART I: Seeking The Call of the Soul.............................1
Chapter 1: The Hunger of the Soul.....................................3
Chapter 2: False Doors, True Longing...............................15
Chapter 3: The Inner Compass...25
Chapter 4: Sacred Curiosity...35

PART II: Finding: Remembering the Inner Source...........47
Chapter 5: The Treasure Within...49
Chapter 6: The Mirror of Creation......................................59
Chapter 7: Integrating Shadow and Light............................69
Chapter 8: The Discipline of Presence...............................81

PART III: Being: Living as Conscious Creator....................93
Chapter 9: The Power of Alignment...................................95
Chapter 10: Choosing Frequencies, Not Outcomes..............103
Chapter 11: The Dance of Co-Creation..............................115
Chapter 12: Embodied Divinity...125

PART IV: Integration: Wholeness in Motion.....................137

Chapter 13: Life as Sacred Spiral............................139

Chapter 14: Freedom Through Self-Honoring....................151

Chapter 15: Seek. Find. Be. 161

Closing Author Note...167

Benediction..169

About the Author...171

A Visual Key to the Journey

Throughout this book, you will encounter simple shapes that
mark the rhythm of the journey.
They are not decorations, but companions—
reminders of truths too deep for words alone,
guiding the subtle movements of *Seek. Find. Be.*

The Circle – Chapter Symbol

A circle greets each chapter,
reminding us that wholeness is always present.
Drawn imperfectly, it honors the beauty of becoming—
complete, yet ever unfinished.
It is the pause before the next step,
the reminder that presence is enough.

The Spiral – Part I: Seeking

The spiral marks the beginning.
It reflects the soul's hunger,
the stirring that pulls us beyond survival.
Its motion turns both inward and outward—
restless, alive, reaching toward mystery.

The Triangle – Part II: Finding

The triangle points upward,
symbolizing clarity and remembrance.
It reminds us of the treasure within,
the light that has always been there.

A shape of ascent,

it reflects the inner turning that reveals what was never lost.

The Diamond (a square turned on its point) – Part III: Being

Balanced and grounded,

the diamond represents alignment.

It speaks of living truth in thought, word, and deed—

not a weight we carry,

but a strength that carries us.

Here, the inner truth finds outward expression.

The Infinity Loop – Part IV: Integration

Flowing endlessly,

the infinity loop embodies wholeness in motion.

It whispers of cycles—

forgetting and remembering,

being and becoming.

Not as contradictions, but as movements of the same life.

It is the eternal dance,

the rhythm of return.

Together: A Quiet Map

Placed side by side,

the circle, spiral, triangle, diamond, and infinity loop

form a symbolic rhythm:

- Each chapter begins in wholeness (Circle).

- Each Part unfolds a new movement of the soul—
  Seeking (Spiral),
  Finding (Triangle),
  Being (Diamond),
  Integrating (Infinity).

They are not instructions, but invitations—
symbols to hold, pause with, and let speak in their own way.
They remind us that the path of the soul is always whole,
not as something finished, but as something alive and
unfolding.

Symbolic Map of the Journey

This map does not chart every step.
It reveals the pattern beneath the steps—
the quiet arc of Seek. Find. Be.
Not as straight lines,
but as living movement.

Like a mirror, it reflects the soul's unfolding.
Like a compass, it points you inward.

Part I – Seeking: The Call of the Soul

Shape: Spiral
The stirring within—the hunger that calls us beyond survival.

- Represents the beginning, the stirring that awakens.
- A movement outward from center, searching, curious, alive.

Part II – Finding: Remembering the Inner Source

Shape: Triangle (upward)
The turning inward—remembering the light already within.

- Represents clarity and alignment.
- The soul lifts upward, recognizing the treasure that was never lost.

Part III – Being: Living as Conscious Creator

Shape: Diamond (square turned on its point)
The grounding—living truth in thought, word, and deed.

- Represents embodiment, stability, and rooted presence.
- The inward truth now seeks expression in the everyday.

Part IV – Integration: Wholeness in Motion

Shape: Infinity Loop (∞)
The eternal rhythm—cycles of forgetting and remembering, being and unfolding.

- Represents the ongoing spiral of life.
- Wholeness is not arrival but continual unfolding.

The Arc of Seek. Find. Be.

Every soul knows the stirring—
the call that whispers of more than survival.
It begins as a hunger,
a spiral of longing that draws us into motion.

In time, we discover
that what we sought has always lived within.
The triangle points upward,
reminding us of the light we carry,
the alignment that comes when we turn inward.

From there, truth seeks embodiment.
The diamond steadies us,
grounding the sacred into thought, word, and deed.
Here, creation is no longer distant—
it becomes a way of being.

Still, the path does not end.
The infinity loop flows on—
cycles of forgetting and remembering,
of seeking, finding, and being again.
This is not failure but rhythm—
the eternal becoming
through which the soul learns its own wholeness.

This is the journey.
Not a line to follow, but a living spiral, a sacred dance.

To seek, to find, to be—
is to awaken to yourself as creator.

Preface

Seek and you remember.
Find and you return.
Be and you create.

Every book carries a seed at its center.
The seed of this one is a question:
What does it mean to live not only as one who awakens and accepts,
but as one who creates consciously, moment by moment?

The earlier books in this series circled around discovery and acceptance—listening for the true self beneath performing, softening into the grace of enoughness. This third book widens the path. It turns toward the quiet but radical possibility that each of us is already a creator, shaping our lives not only through what we do, but through what we embody.

Creation is often imagined as something extraordinary—art hung in galleries, innovations that change the world, legacies written in stone. Yet the soul whispers of another truth:
that every breath is an act of creation.

Every thought, every word, every gesture of presence shapes the world around us.

What we seek in greatness is already alive in the ordinary.

I do not write this book as one who has mastered the art of conscious creation. I write as one who has listened, stumbled, found my way back, and remembered—again and again. What I offer here are not conclusions, but companions for the path: reflections meant to stir what is already waiting within you.

This book continues the rhythm woven through this trilogy:

Seek. Find. Be.

- **Seek**—the awakening of longing, the inner call to question the stories that bind you and to listen for the deeper truth beneath the noise.
- **Find**—the remembrance of what rises from within, the unveiling of your own essence, the recognition of the light you have always carried.
- **Be**—the embodiment of your truth, the quiet courage to live in alignment with your soul's knowing, to create from wholeness rather than fear.

These are not steps to master, but movements of the soul—
spiral, rhythmic, alive.
You may circle back to familiar ground with new eyes
or leap forward into uncharted depths.
Wherever you find yourself in this rhythm,
you are not late to your own becoming,
and you are not alone.

This book is not a manual.
It is not a prescription.
It is a mirror.

The words here are seeds;
you may plant them where you wish,
water them with your own experience,
and let them grow in their own time.

As you turn these pages,
may you find yourself both seeker and creator—
both student and teacher
of your own becoming.

May you remember
that to know thyself
is not only to discover and accept,
but to shape,
to birth,
and to live
as the creator you already are.

Kea Rivers

And so the spiral stirs…
calling you inward to begin again.

Part I - Seeking: The Call of the Soul

The stirring within—
the hunger that calls us beyond survival.

Chapter 1

The Hunger of the Soul

What you seek is seeking you.
—Rumi

There is a hunger that no meal can satisfy, no achievement can quiet, no relationship can fully soothe. It stirs when the lights go dim and the noise of the day finally falls away. For a moment, you hear it—not as a voice, but as a pull.

This is where the journey begins—not with answers, but with the first stirring of awareness.

What we often interpret as something missing is something else entirely. This hunger is not a verdict against your life. It is the soul's reminder that survival is not enough. We can build lives filled with accomplishment—careers, families, recognition, security—and still feel an unnamable stirring beneath it all. We can climb ladders, collect titles, surround ourselves with comforts, and still discover that the hunger lingers.

Not to shame us, but to wake us.

This hunger does not arise from what is missing in our lives, but from something within us beginning to remember itself. It is not absence, but a threshold.

Every culture, every age has known this inner stirring. Some have called it the search for God, others the quest for meaning, others simply the longing for "something more." Whatever name we give it, the essence remains: the soul refuses to be muted by survival alone.

The hunger often first appears as dissatisfaction, though it rarely introduces itself so plainly. Sometimes it slips in quietly, like a whisper beneath ordinary life: *Is this all there is?* Other times it rises with force, like a storm that shakes the foundations of what once felt secure. In either form, it unsettles the ground beneath us.

So we try to answer it with more of what we already know. More work. More effort. More affirmation. More distraction. Yet no matter how much we collect or achieve, the hunger deepens—because its origin is not in the body or the mind.

It is in the soul.

This hunger is not here to harm us, though it can feel unsettling. It is not a flaw to eliminate, but a passage to move through. When we dare to listen, it begins to change shape. What felt like emptiness begins to reveal itself as a threshold.

You may notice it in the spaces between tasks, when the rush of the day pauses and silence grows louder—moments when forgetting loosens its grip and something deeper has room to surface. You may notice it at a milestone—the degree, the promotion, the house, the relationship—when celebration feels strangely thin. Or you may feel it in your body: a heaviness in the chest, a deep stirring in the gut, as though something within you is quietly insisting, *Remember*.

What is being remembered was never lost—only overlooked.

When we are willing to listen, the hunger of the soul can become a teacher. It unsettles us so we will not remain asleep. It disrupts what is comfortable so we may turn toward what is true. It whispers not of something missing, but of something more real waiting to be lived.

So the journey begins—not because you are incomplete, but because something within you is waking. What we sometimes mistake as "something wrong" is often the first signal of something deeper: life calling you inward, back toward your own essence.

What shape does this hunger take in you? Where does it rise— in the quiet moments, the unguarded hours, the unspoken desires? If you pause long enough to listen, you may find that the hunger itself is the first gift: the call that invites you toward who you have always been.

The Stirring Beneath Achievement

When we do not yet recognize this hunger as a call from within, we learn to interpret it as an emptiness that must be filled from the outside. The world tells us that if we work hard enough, rise high enough, or gather enough recognition, we will finally feel complete. So we turn outward. We set goals, pursue promotions, earn degrees, cultivate relationships, and collect the markers of success. Each new accomplishment seems to promise a kind of settling—a reassurance that we are "enough" by the measures that surround us.

For a time, it can feel true. The thrill of success brings a surge of validation—relief, satisfaction, even belonging. The affirmation of others washes over us with warmth, and for a moment we feel seen and steady. A new title, a new home, a new circle of belonging in the world—these things can soothe the hunger for a while. We tell ourselves, *This is it. This is what I've been searching for.*

But sooner or later, the familiar stirring returns. The applause fades. The degree hangs on the wall. The title becomes part of the email signature. The home settles into ordinary days of dust and laundry. What once felt like arrival becomes the new normal—and beneath it, the deeper pull remains.

This is a truth we often hesitate to admit: even in our moments of greatest achievement, the hunger of the soul can remain. We cross one finish line only to find another race waiting. We reach a summit only to discover the view is not as complete as we imagined. The sense of fulfillment is real, but it does not last.

Perhaps this is not a flaw in us.

Perhaps it is design.

The hunger beneath achievement does not arise to diminish what we have gained. It does not declare that success or milestones are meaningless. It simply reminds us that these things were never meant to nourish the soul in full. They can bring happiness. They can mark growth. They can hold beauty. But they cannot answer the deeper call that asks—not *What have you done?* but *Who are you learning to embody?*

Think back on a time you reached something you had long desired. Did the celebration last forever? Or did the deeper stirring return once the moment passed? That stirring is not emptiness—it is a threshold. It is the soul reminding us that life is more than accomplishment. It asks us to look beyond what we have achieved to what still calls us forward.

The stirring beneath achievement is not a sign that you are ungrateful or "never satisfied." It is the soul's steady refusal to settle for surface fulfillment. It is a sacred insistence that keeps asking for aliveness, not merely success—so that we do not confuse the ladder with the horizon.

So achievement becomes a paradox. It gives us reason to celebrate, and yet it can also awaken us. It shows us both what is possible and what is still unfolding. In this way, even achievement can become a teacher—revealing that the hunger of the soul cannot be fulfilled by success alone.

If achievement cannot silence the hunger, then what is it

pointing us toward? Perhaps the longing itself is asking us to look deeper—beyond survival, beyond accomplishment, beyond the surface of a life that only appears full.

We feel this hunger as longing—not pain, but an inner pull toward what is more essential, more alive within us.

And beneath all our efforts to prove ourselves lies a more honest question:

Are we truly alive, or are we merely surviving?

The Difference Between Survival and Aliveness

Survival is necessary. It keeps us moving through the demands of daily life—earning a living, paying the bills, caring for family, managing responsibilities. It builds the structures that sustain us and the routines that help us endure. Without survival, life itself would not continue.

But survival, on its own, is not enough.

We can survive for years—even decades—without ever truly feeling alive. We can meet every external measure of success and still sense that something essential is missing. The hunger of the soul exposes this difference—not to condemn us, but to invite us deeper into being human: not merely functioning within life, but awakening within it.

Aliveness is something altogether different. It is not measured by accomplishment or possessions, but by depth of presence—by how fully we inhabit our own lives rather than merely moving through them. It is the difference between living in a haze of constant activity and waking each day with a sense of wonder. Aliveness arises when we live not only to meet obligations, but to answer the deeper call within.

We often glimpse aliveness in fleeting moments: standing in awe before a sunrise, laughing so freely that time disappears, creating something that feels as though it flows through us rather than from us. In such moments, life feels charged with meaning, and the boundary between the ordinary and the sacred seems to soften.

These moments reveal a quiet contrast within us—the difference between surviving and being fully alive.

Survival asks, *What must I do to get through today?*
Aliveness asks, *What is waiting to be awakened in me today?*

Survival focuses on safety, stability, predictability. Aliveness invites risk—not recklessness, but the willingness to follow the deeper pull of the soul, even when the path ahead is unclear. Survival builds walls; aliveness opens doors. Survival ensures that we endure; aliveness ensures that we become more fully ourselves.

Beneath achievement often lies a longing for aliveness. It is the part of us that refuses to settle for mere existence. It will not be satisfied by more hours at the office, another line on the resume, or another box checked off the list. It calls us beyond comfort and into wonder, beyond repetition and into possibility.

To choose aliveness does not mean rejecting survival. We still need food, shelter, community, and the rhythms that sustain us—the cycles of effort and rest, holding on and letting go. But when survival becomes the whole story, something within us begins to stir.

Aliveness restores balance. It reminds us that life is not only something to endure—it is something to be experienced, felt, and lived from the inside out, guided not only by obligation, but by inner awareness.

When we are willing to listen, hunger can become a teacher. It reveals the gap between surviving and living, between existing and awakening. It points us toward a life where depth matters as much as duty, where wonder has as much claim on us as responsibility.

For in the end, it is not enough to survive.

The soul longs to be alive.

If survival alone cannot satisfy and achievement does not settle us, then what is the hunger of the soul truly asking of us? Perhaps it is not here to be silenced at all. Perhaps longing is not a sign of absence, but a signal of the soul—a quiet remembering of something more.

For beneath every stirring is an opening—one that draws us beyond the surface of life and into its depths. Longing does not arise to unsettle us, but to guide us.

The Invitation Hidden in Longing

Longing is often misunderstood. We treat it as evidence of emptiness, as proof that something is wrong with us or missing from our lives. We try to fill it, fix it, or push it away. We move faster, work harder, and seek more desperately—hoping the inner stirring within us will finally fade. But what if longing is not absence at all? What if it is presence in disguise—the soul's way of pointing us toward what is most real?

Every longing carries within it a spark of remembrance. The longing for love reminds us that we are made for connection. The longing for purpose stirs us to remember that our lives are meant to matter. The longing for freedom awakens the truth that the soul cannot thrive under chains of pretense or fear. Even outward-facing longings—for success, approval, or "more"—can teach us something. They reveal, often through disappointment, that the surface cannot satisfy what only depth can nourish.

Longing unsettles because it refuses to let us remain where we are. It stirs when we have stayed too long in places that have grown too small for us. It rises when we shrink ourselves into

11

roles that cannot hold our wholeness. It grows louder when we ignore its whisper—pressing on with survival and achievement while something deeper waits, quietly calling us back.

Longing is not here to shame us. It does not arrive as judgment, but as possibility. It opens an inner threshold and asks us to consider: *What if there is more to me than I have yet allowed myself to live?* The opening within us is not emptiness, but space— room being made within us for what is truer, deeper, more alive.

Think of a time you felt a longing that would not leave you. Perhaps it rose in quiet moments, when the surface noise paused and silence grew heavy. Perhaps it appeared at the peak of accomplishment, when the applause faded and you found yourself asking, *Is this the limit of who I am?*

That lingering pull was not a sign that something had ended, but that something deeper was beginning.

It was a summons—the soul drawing you closer to your own essence.

To accept the calling hidden in longing is not to rush toward answers, but to remain with the question long enough to hear its deeper truth. Longing stretches us, but in stretching, it opens us. What once felt like a restless stirring begins to reveal itself as direction. What once felt like absence begins to shimmer with presence.

The hunger of the soul is not something to be resolved, but something to be followed. Longing is one way that hunger speaks—the voice that calls us beyond survival, beyond achievement, into the possibility of a life not merely endured, but fully lived.

Closing Reflection

The hunger of the soul is not an error. It is not evidence that something is amiss, nor a sign that you have strayed from your path. It is the beginning of awareness—the moment survival is no longer enough, the moment the soul begins to stir.

This hunger invites us to notice the difference between existing and being fully alive. It calls us beyond surface fulfillment toward a deeper nourishment—the kind that expands our awareness and draws us closer to our essence. What we often experience as inner agitation is not emptiness, but movement: the soul remembering itself.

Every stirring, every quiet sense that something more is possible, is an opening. Longing is not suffering, but orientation—the soul's way of pointing us toward what is more alive and true. It draws us toward a life that is not merely endured, but consciously lived.

The hunger, then, is not something to quiet or suppress. It is the beginning of the journey. It is the soul knocking at the door of our awareness, asking us to listen. When we dare to pause and hear it, what once felt like disquiet becomes the first step toward home.

To seek is not to confess something lacking, but to respond to what is already alive within us. It is to trust that what stirs in us is not confusion, but guidance.

So we turn now from hunger to the search it awakens. From the first stirring of awareness to the paths we begin to explore. For every seeker starts by looking outward—and only later discovers that what they long for has always been waiting within.

Chapter 2

False Doors, True Longing

You wander from room to room, hunting for the diamond necklace
that is already around your neck.
—Rumi

The hunger of the soul does not leave us still. It awakens movement. It stirs us toward something we cannot yet name, yet somehow recognize as essential.

When we first begin to seek, we almost always look outward. We search using the maps we have inherited, the roles we have learned to inhabit, the stories we have been taught to trust. What we call seeking is often the soul's first attempt to understand its own hunger. We turn toward the doors the world assures us will lead to fulfillment—achievement, belonging, validation, stability. These doors are familiar, and for a time, they may even open into spaces that feel full.

But sooner or later, we begin to notice that not every door leads where we imagined. Some open into rooms that shine brightly at first, only to dim with time. Others lead into long corridors of accomplishment where one milestone follows another, yet something within us remains unsatisfied. Still others promise connection but offer belonging that depends on shrinking, performing, or conforming.

Here we encounter the paradox of seeking: the soul's hunger is

15

real, but our earliest responses to it are shaped by what we have learned to desire. We move toward what culture celebrates — the next title, the ideal relationship, the polished image, the curated life that signals worth. We move from door to door, trusting that fulfillment must be waiting just beyond the next threshold.

Yet when the door finally opens, we often find only a brief sense of completion, followed by a familiar whisper:
Is this really the limit of who I am?

To call these doors "false" is not to dismiss them. Achievement, belonging, validation, and certainty all carry value. They are not illusions. But they cannot fulfill what they were never designed to hold. They were never meant to carry the full weight of the soul's longing.

The gift of the false door is that it reveals what cannot sustain us, so we can begin to recognize what might. Each moment of disillusionment, each quiet return of hunger, is not a setback but instruction. It teaches us that longing itself is trustworthy, even when the answers we first pursue are not.

So the journey deepens. We begin to sense that longing is not something to suppress, but something to listen to. The hunger does not deceive us; it guides us. Even when we knock on doors that cannot hold what we seek, the inner pull continues to point us toward a deeper home.

When the hunger first awakens, our attention turns outward. We reach for what is visible, measurable, and affirmed by others. Roles, relationships, achievements, and identities become the places we believe will settle the inner stirring.

This is where seeking often begins: in the pursuit of fulfillment through externals.

The Search for Fulfillment in Externals

When the hunger of the soul stirs, our instinct is to scan the outer edges of life, asking: *Where can I find what is missing?* The world offers no shortage of answers. Status, connection, recognition, security — each promises wholeness, each beckons with the allure of satisfaction just within reach.

So we invest ourselves in these pursuits. We pour energy into work, hoping accomplishment will confirm our worth. We reach toward intimacy, believing another person will complete us. We seek affirmation, imagining that enough approval will quiet the inner stirring. We gather experiences and symbols of success, hoping the fullness of our lives will echo as fullness within.

For a time, these pursuits can feel convincing. The promotion brings a surge of meaning. The relationship glows with possibility. Recognition feels intoxicating. The hunger seems softened, as though we have finally discovered what we were looking for.

17

But beneath the surface, something remains awake. The applause fades. The novelty wears thin. What once felt complete begins to feel strangely hollow. And again, we find ourselves unsettled, wondering why satisfaction does not last.

Here we encounter another paradox: external fulfillment can nourish parts of us, but it cannot sustain the whole of us. The soul does not live on applause or outward markers of success. Status and image may support us, but they cannot anchor us. At best, they offer brief reassurance. At worst, they distract us from listening to the deeper call within.

Yet even here, there is hidden grace. False doors remain teachers. Each moment of dissatisfaction carries a message: what we truly seek cannot be handed to us by the world. External achievements may point toward growth, but they cannot replace the deeper recognition of self.

The search for fulfillment in externals is not wasted. It is part of the human journey—a stage we are meant to pass through. Through experience, not theory, we begin to understand that the hunger of the soul cannot be answered by anything less than truth. Longing endures not to unsettle us, but to guide us toward a deeper homecoming.

Slowly, we begin to notice that what we pursue outside often reflects what is awakening within. The soul does not reject our search; it waits patiently, whispering through unmet desires: *Look deeper. What you seek is already yours.*

Achievement, belonging, affirmation, and stability each hold beauty and meaning. Yet eventually, a moment arrives when the silence after the applause feels louder than the applause itself. The newness fades. The fullness thins. And again, the quiet stirring returns.

It is in this moment—when outward answers no longer satisfy—that something deeper begins to awaken within us.

The Moment Externals Prove Insufficient

There comes a moment when the shine wears off. The promotion that once felt like a summit begins to feel like another plateau. The relationship that promised completion reveals its limits. The possessions that once sparked joy fade into the background of everyday life. What once seemed like enough no longer holds the same weight.

This moment may arrive gently, like a whisper rising when outer noise subsides: *This cannot be all there is.* Or it may arrive suddenly, disrupting the structures we once relied upon. However it comes, the message is the same: externals, though meaningful, cannot carry the full depth of the soul's longing.

At first, we often resist this realization. We add more to our calendars, pursue the next milestone, seek greater affirmation. We tell ourselves that the next achievement will finally bring peace. Yet no matter how much we accumulate or accomplish, the subtle stirring returns.

What returns is not disappointment, but awareness. The hunger beneath our successes is not there to diminish what we have achieved, but to remind us that the soul cannot be sustained by externals alone. Love, work, recognition, and beauty matter. Yet they are not ultimate. They were never designed to satisfy the deepest call within us.

When externals lose their power to reassure us, the experience can feel disorienting. The goals we pursued, the roles we inhabited, the markers of success we trusted—they no longer quiet the questions beneath them. Yet within this disruption, something unexpected begins to emerge: clarity.

We begin to sense that what we are looking for cannot be measured, displayed, or acquired. For many, this realization feels less like discovering something new and more like reconnecting with something already present—a sense of meaning, coherence, or inner truth that had been overshadowed by outward pursuits.

Paradoxically, this moment is a gift. Until externals reveal their limits, we may never learn to look elsewhere. The recurring inner stirring teaches us that fulfillment cannot be sustained by outward achievements alone. The journey toward wholeness does not begin outside us.

It begins within.

So the false doors close, one by one—not to imprison us, but to redirect us. Not to judge us, but to guide us back to what the soul has always known: what we hunger for is not out there, but within.

Even when externals lose their shine, the hunger does not disappear. Something deeper remains.

The Deeper Whisper That Remains

When the noise of achievement fades and the comfort of externals thins, the inner voice becomes clearer. Beneath applause, possessions, and roles, something steady begins to speak.

This whisper is not loud. It does not command. It does not hurry. It remains—patient, persistent, quietly present in the spaces between distractions. It rises when the party ends, when the inbox is empty, when the constant motion pauses and we notice what has been there all along.

We may try to cover it with more activity, more noise, more proof. We may layer over it with ambition or bury it beneath busyness. But no matter how much we add, the whisper continues. Not as accusation, but as invitation. Not as judgment, but as remembrance.

At first, we may misinterpret it. We may mistake it for emptiness or uncertainty. Yet the longer we listen, the more we realize it is not absence at all. It is presence—the quiet intelligence of the soul refusing to let us trade depth for distraction.

The deeper whisper runs through every longing. It speaks through joy, reminding us of what resonates as true. It speaks through dissatisfaction, teaching us that what we reached for cannot sustain us. It speaks through inner stirring, pointing us beyond the surface toward the depths within.

If we listen closely, we begin to recognize how constant it has been. In childhood wonder. In moments of loss. In seasons of accomplishment. Always waiting. Always guiding. Always pointing.

This is why the hunger cannot be silenced by externals. This is why satisfaction fades. This is why longing endures. Because what we seek has never been "out there."
It has always been here—within us,
waiting to be remembered.

When we finally allow ourselves to hear the whisper, something shifts. We are no longer trying to quiet the hunger through externals. We are beginning to listen.

And in listening, we discover direction.

The whisper becomes the compass of the soul—guiding us not with certainty, but with orientation. It does not reveal the whole path at once, but it always points toward home.

Closing Reflection

The journey of seeking so often begins with reaching outward. We knock on the doors the world celebrates—achievement, recognition, success, security. For a time, these doors offer something real. They bring meaning, beauty, and glimpses of fulfillment. But sooner or later, each door reveals its limits. The applause fades. The roles we inhabit cannot hold the full depth of our longing. Still, the hunger remains.

This return of hunger is a moment of recognition. It reveals what externals cannot provide: enduring meaning, inner coherence, and authentic truth. Longing persists because something deeper within us is coming awake.

False doors are not wasted. Each one teaches us something essential. They help us discern between temporary reassurance and what can truly hold us. Through them, we learn—slowly, honestly—that fulfillment cannot be found outside us alone.

Through it all, the deeper whisper remains.
Steady. Patient. Persistent.
It speaks through inner stirring, reminding us that comfort without meaning cannot sustain the soul. It speaks through joy, hinting at what feels most alive within us. It speaks in silence, steady beneath the noise of expectation.

The whisper honors our searching. For every attempt to find meaning brings us closer to a turning point: the realization that what we seek outwardly may be calling us inward.

So the movement of seeking begins to change.

We are no longer searching only in the world around us.
We begin, slowly and quietly, to listen within.

Here, the journey shifts—
from searching for answers to sensing direction,
from outward pursuit to inner attunement.

Hunger becomes something to understand rather than escape.
The whisper becomes less something to quiet and more a guide.

What we seek has not disappeared.
It has been waiting—
within us all along.

Chapter 3

The Inner Compass

At the center of your being you have the answer;
you know who you are and you know what you want.
— Lao Tzu

When the false doors close and the externals prove insufficient, we are left with a quieter, more unsettling call: to turn inward. What once felt like disappointment begins to reveal itself as guidance. The hunger that refuses to leave is not a void to be filled, but a signal to be followed. At the heart of this signal lies something steady, something constant—something that has been with us all along: the inner compass.

What begins as hunger often deepens into longing.
Longing, when listened to, becomes desire.
And desire, when trusted, reveals direction.

Unlike the externals, which shift with circumstance, the inner compass does not fade. It is not swayed by applause, diminished by setbacks, or dependent on outcomes. Its language is subtle—more whisper than command, more pull than push—but once we learn to recognize it, its direction becomes unmistakable.

The compass of the soul does not speak in straight lines or detailed maps. It speaks in nudges, stirrings, resonances—the

25

sense of rightness we cannot fully explain, the felt misalignment that alerts us when we are no longer living in resonance. It shows itself in longings that endure, in clarity that arises naturally, in the peace that lingers when we choose the path that feels true.

Many of us have been taught to distrust this compass. We've been told to defer to logic, to authority, to what is visible and measurable. Desire has often been cast as unreliable, longing dismissed as something to outgrow, intuition overlooked as inconsistent or unprovable. Yet beneath all of this conditioning, the compass remains. Waiting. Pointing. Calling us back to ourselves.

To follow your inner compass is not to reject the world, but to listen more deeply within it. It is to integrate them into a deeper trust: that the soul carries within it a knowing that cannot be silenced. The compass does not demand that you see the whole path; it asks only that you trust the next step.

This chapter is about remembering that the compass is real—and learning to listen for its direction. For if the hunger is the invitation, and longing the threshold, then the compass is the guide that leads us home.

If the inner compass is real, how does it speak? Its language often begins in desire—those steady pulls, those persistent longings, those moments of resonance that light something within us. For too long, many of us have been taught to distrust desire, to treat it as misleading or something to restrain. But what if desire is not meant to lead us astray, but to point us toward the path of becoming?

This is where the compass first begins to guide:
in the recognition that desire is directional, not deceptive.

Desire as Directional, Not Deceptive

Desire has long carried a complicated reputation. Across cultures and spiritual traditions, we have often been taught to distrust it—to see desire as untrustworthy, selfish, or misleading. Many of us learned to silence what we want, fearing that longing would pull us away from responsibility, truth, or goodness.

Yet not all desire is the same.

Some desires arise from fear, comparison, or conditioning— impulses shaped by survival, status, or the need for approval. These wants can be urgent, fleeting, or compulsive. They often promise quick satisfaction, yet leave us feeling unsettled once more.

But beneath these surface wants, however, lies another kind of desire—subtler, steadier, and more enduring.

This deeper longing does not demand attention. It returns gently across seasons of life. It is the pull toward beauty, freedom, creativity, connection, meaning, and wholeness—not as things to acquire, but as ways of being. Such longing does not feel like craving; it feels like recognition.

In this sense, desire is not merely appetite. It is signal.
It stirs when our outer lives no longer reflect our inner truth. It awakens when the roles we inhabit begin to feel too small for who we are becoming. It draws us not toward excess, but toward coherence—a deeper alignment between what we live and what we are.

To recognize desire in this way is not to indulge every impulse, but to listen more discerningly. Beneath surface wants lies a subtler voice—one that does not demand, but invites. These are the desires that persist even when we try to ignore them, the ones that resurface in moments of quiet, the ones that, when honored, bring not just pleasure, but a sense of resonance—a feeling of rightness, of coming into alignment with ourselves.

When we begin to notice this distinction, desire no longer appears as an enemy of truth. It becomes a form of guidance. Not every desire is a compass, but some are. And learning to sense the difference is part of the journey of remembering who we are.

If desire is not merely wanting, but signal, then the hunger we feel is not evidence of emptiness. It is evidence of movement— life within us seeking meaning, coherence, and depth.

And when a signal endures, it begins to reveal something more than feeling.

It begins to reveal direction.

The Soul's Way of Pointing Home

When desire endures, it does not merely ask for attention—it begins to orient us.

Some longings skim the surface of our lives. Others remain, quietly shaping the horizon of who we are becoming. These enduring longings are not accidents. They arise from something essential within us, something that remembers what we sometimes forget.

When we look closely, we begin to sense that each lasting longing carries a movement within it—a subtle pull toward wholeness.

Longing carries information. When we long for freedom, it is because something in us remembers a way of being beyond fear or expectation. When we long for love, it is because connection is not foreign to us—it is native. It arises from our design, not our deserving.

The pull toward creativity reflects an inner current that seeks expression, not for applause, but for authenticity. Even the desire for rest is not withdrawal from life, but a return to its natural rhythm.

Yet we often misinterpret these signals. We assume they point us outward—toward the perfect partner, the ideal career, the flawless version of ourselves. External forms may mirror our longings and sometimes help us take the next step, but they are not the destination. Beneath every form lies a deeper essence that does not change.

This is why enduring longings persist. We may distract ourselves, bury our inner stirrings beneath busyness, or cover them with achievement, but they return — not to accuse us, but to remind us of what we have not yet fully claimed.

To follow these longings does not mean pursuing what the world defines as success. More often, it means listening beneath appearances — asking what each desire is truly pointing toward. When we learn to listen in this way, desire becomes more than impulse. It becomes orientation.

And orientation, over time, becomes something steadier than feeling.

It becomes a compass.

In this sense, the soul does not push us forward so much as it draws us inward. It remembers for us. And in remembering, it quietly points us home.

To sense this pull is only the beginning.
To trust it requires courage — the willingness to believe that the quiet inner movement is not deception, but direction.

Trusting the Quiet Pull

The soul does not always speak in pronouncement. More often, it speaks in whispers — a subtle knowing, a quiet tug, a gentle sense that something within us is asking to be heard. It does not command or compel itself; it invites.

At first, we may doubt this invitation. In a world shaped by insistent expectations and urgent voices, the quiet pull can seem easy to dismiss. Yet it endures. Long after the noise fades, it remains—waiting for us to listen.

Trusting this pull can feel uncertain, even risky. We are trained to seek clarity before movement: proof, plans, outcomes we can measure. The soul offers no such guarantees. Its guidance arrives not as a complete map, but as a single step illuminated in low light. To trust the pull is to walk by this softer guidance, believing that the next step is enough.

The quiet pull often reveals itself in ordinary, intimate ways. It may appear as the heaviness of remaining in a role, relationship, or identity that no longer fits. It may arise as subtle resistance—an inner friction that grows when we ignore what wants to emerge. Or it may appear as a quiet joy, a sense of expansion when we lean toward what feels deeply true, even when it defies explanation. The pull does not pressure us forward, but it does not disappear.

To honor it requires courage. Sometimes it means loosening our attachment to what is familiar. Sometimes it means disappointing expectations, including our own. Sometimes it means saying yes to an inner knowing that cannot yet be justified, but feels unmistakably alive. Trusting the quiet pull is rarely the easiest choice, but it is often the most honest one.

Yet this trust is not blind. It does not dismiss reason or wisdom; it deepens them. It recognizes that logic alone cannot chart the terrain of the soul, and that inner knowing and outer understanding are meant to work together. To trust the quiet pull is not to abandon discernment, but to expand it.

Over time, listening becomes less frightening. We begin to notice how honoring the pull opens doors we could not have forced, how unexpected connections arise, how even uncertainty can feel strangely aligned when we are in resonance with ourselves. What once felt risky begins to feel like coherence. What once felt unclear begins to feel necessary.

The hunger of the soul brought us to listening. Desire revealed itself as direction. Now trust becomes the bridge—the moment when inner direction becomes lived movement.

Closing Reflection

The soul does not leave us without guidance. What begins as hunger becomes longing, what longing reveals becomes desire, and within desire we begin to sense direction. Beneath it all, the compass has been steady, whispering in ways too subtle to ignore for long. To listen is one step. To trust is another. And it is trust that transforms the whisper from a distant echo into a living path.

Trusting the quiet pull does not promise certainty. It does not offer the full map, laid out from beginning to end. It gives only enough light for the next step. At first, this can feel unsettling.

We crave guarantees, evidence, outcomes. But the soul invites us to walk differently—guided not by proof alone, but by resonance, by the inner sense of rightness that defies explanation yet feels undeniably true.

Each time we honor the pull, something shifts. Possibilities open where we once felt confined. Encounters arise that could not have been planned. Even in uncertainty, a strange steadiness emerges, as though life itself is aligning with our inner truth. We begin to see that the quiet pull was never random. It was always the compass pointing us toward what is real.

This is the work of remembrance: recognizing that what stirs within us is not emptiness, but an opening. That desire is not deception, but direction. That the pull we feel is not confusion, but wisdom. Each enduring longing carries the imprint of home. Each step taken in trust leads us deeper into the truth we have always carried within.

Trust, however, is not the destination. It is the turning point. To live by the compass is not to control the path, but to remain open to it—to walk with curiosity, humility, and wonder into what unfolds. The soul does not hand us a finished script. It invites us into a living conversation, one step at a time.

And here, the journey bends again. Having learned to trust the compass, we are invited into something new—not certainty, but curiosity; not answers, but discovery. For the compass points the way, but it is curiosity that opens us to what the path is ready to reveal.

Chapter 4

Sacred Curiosity

Wonder is the beginning of wisdom.
— *Socrates*

Trust opens the door, but curiosity is what allows us to step through. When we begin to honor the quiet pull of the soul, something in us shifts. We move from needing certainty to cultivating openness, from demanding answers to allowing discovery. Curiosity becomes the posture that makes the journey possible.

Many of us are taught to approach life as a terrain to navigate, a path to master, a future to control. We seek guarantees before we move, clarity before we risk, outcomes before we trust. Yet the soul speaks in a different rhythm. It does not offer finished maps; it invites us into unfolding.

Sacred curiosity is not an impulsive hunger for novelty. It is not distraction, nor escape. It is the quiet willingness to meet life as it is—to lean toward mystery with trust rather than resistance. It asks not, *How do I control this?* but *What might this be revealing?*

To walk with curiosity is to treat life as a conversation with the unseen. It means loosening our grip on certainty and letting wonder take its place. It means standing in the "not yet known" without panic, trusting that the compass is still guiding us, even when we cannot see the full landscape.

Curiosity changes the way we move through our lives. Instead of rushing to explain, manage, or control, we begin to listen. The unknown becomes not an obstacle to overcome, but a space where something new may be born.

This chapter is an invitation to reclaim curiosity—not as weakness, but as reverence; not as indecision, but as courage. For it is curiosity that keeps us open enough to receive what the journey is already trying to reveal.

But curiosity is not only a way of seeing. It is a way of walking —especially when the path ahead is unclear.

Entering the Unknown Without Demand

To live with sacred curiosity is to loosen our insistence on certainty. We are conditioned to believe that clarity must come before movement, that answers must precede action, that safety must be secured before we take a step. Yet the soul rarely speaks in guarantees. It speaks in invitations.

Entering the unknown without demand does not mean walking blindly or abandoning discernment. It means releasing the belief that we must understand everything before we are allowed to begin. It is the willingness to move without forcing the path to reveal itself all at once.

The unknown is not an absence of meaning.

It is a space where meaning is still unfolding.

So much of our anxiety comes not from danger, but from uncertainty. We are taught to equate the unknown with threat, unpredictability with failure, and mystery with loss of control.

Yet life itself is not built on certainty. It is built on emergence. Growth does not arrive fully formed; it reveals itself gradually, through moments we cannot predict or plan.

When we demand certainty, we shrink the unknown into something manageable. We reduce its vastness to fit our expectations. We try to tame what is meant to transform us. In doing so, we close ourselves to possibilities we could not have imagined.

But when we enter the unknown without demand, something shifts. We stop trying to dominate the mystery and begin to participate in it.

The closed door becomes a turning rather than an ending.
The delay becomes a gestation rather than a denial.
The uncertainty becomes a threshold rather than a void.

Curiosity allows us to remain present in this threshold. It does not erase fear, but it gives fear a wider container. We learn to hold uncertainty without collapsing into it. We discover that not knowing is not the same as being lost.

To enter the unknown without demand is to treat life as a

dialogue rather than a problem to solve. It is to trust that each step, however partial, carries intelligence within it. It is to believe that the inner compass does not disappear simply because the terrain is unfamiliar.

The soul does not ask us to see the whole path.
It asks us to stay awake to the next movement.

In this posture, the unknown ceases to be an enemy. It becomes a living field—a place where transformation is possible precisely because it has not yet been defined. What once felt like disorientation begins to feel like spaciousness. What once felt unsettling begins to feel like opening.

When we stop demanding certainty, we begin to sense that life is not withholding answers from us. It is inviting us into deeper participation.

In that participation, curiosity becomes more than a posture. It becomes a way of walking. In this way, curiosity shifts from a momentary response to uncertainty into something more enduring—a presence that accompanies us as we move through what we cannot yet name.

Curiosity as a Sacred Companion

When certainty loosens its grip, curiosity steps forward—not as a distraction, but as a presence. It does not demand answers or rush toward conclusions. Instead, it walks beside us, reminding us that the unknown is not something to fear, but something to enter with openness.

Curiosity changes how we meet life. Where fear sees threat, curiosity asks a question. Where disappointment feels like an ending, curiosity wonders what might now begin. Where delay tempts us into frustration, curiosity imagines what unseen work might be quietly unfolding beneath the surface. The circumstances themselves may not change, but our relationship to them does. We soften. We widen. We begin to sense possibility where we once felt only limitation.

As a companion, curiosity does not require us to be certain or complete. It meets us precisely in the places where clarity is absent. It whispers: *Stay with this moment. Do not rush past it. Something is here for you.* In this way, curiosity keeps us from collapsing into despair or hardening into control. It teaches us to remain receptive—to life, to meaning, to the subtle movements of the soul.

Curiosity also reshapes how we relate to ourselves. Instead of treating doubt as something to overcome or uncertainty as a sign of misdirection, we begin to honor them as natural companions on the journey. Questions become expressions of aliveness, not evidence that we have lost our way. The unknown shifts from being a threat to faith into the very ground where trust can deepen. We give ourselves permission to be learners again—open to being surprised, humble enough to be changed.

Over time, curiosity becomes more than a response to uncertainty. It becomes a way of inhabiting the world. It steadies us in seasons of transition and keeps us from rushing past the quiet teachings hidden in waiting or silence. It reminds us that life is not only about what we are moving toward, but about what is already present and quietly taking shape.

Seen this way, curiosity is no longer merely a question—it is a form of reverence. It honors mystery without trying to control it. It meets life as it is, even when it arrives in unfamiliar forms. The unknown ceases to feel like emptiness and begins to reveal itself as a living field—fertile with possibility, alive with becoming.

As curiosity walks beside us, something gently shifts. The impulse to push the path forward begins to soften. We sense that the journey does not need to be mastered—only entered.

When curiosity becomes a companion rather than a reflux, the urgency to control what comes next loosens its grip. We begin to trust that the path does not need to be fully understood before it can be lived. Something in us relaxes, making room for a different way of moving forward—not through certainty, but through unfolding.

Letting the Path Unfold

Curiosity eventually teaches us something subtler and deeper than explanation: patience with what we cannot yet see. Instead of pressing for answers, we begin to notice the rhythm of life itself—unfolding step by step, moment by moment, according to a timing wiser than our own.

The soul rarely reveals the full picture in advance. Perhaps it cannot. Or perhaps it does not need to. What we call uncertainty may not be a flaw in the journey, but a form of care—a way of ensuring that growth unfolds gradually, in proportion to our readiness. The path becomes visible as we are able to walk it.

To let the path unfold is to loosen our grip on control. It is to accept that not everything can be rushed, engineered, or predicted. It is to make room for synchronicities that cannot be planned, lessons that arrive indirectly, and insights that surface only after long seasons of waiting. The soul does not move by deadlines or straight lines. It moves by seasons, by spirals, by subtle thresholds of becoming.

There is a hidden wisdom in this unfolding. A seed does not bloom by command; it opens when the conditions are right. A river does not rush to its end; it shapes itself patiently around every stone and curve. So too with us. What feels like delay may be preparation. What feels like detour may be protection. What feels like emptiness may be the fertile ground in which something new is quietly taking root.

When we try to force the path, we often miss what is already present. We hurry past the subtle lessons hidden in waiting, overlook the small revelations woven into ordinary days, and dismiss the quiet moments that carry more truth than dramatic breakthroughs. But when we allow the path to unfold, we begin to sense that nothing is wasted. Even uncertainty belongs. Even slowness has meaning. Even the unseen is shaping us.

Letting the path unfold is not passivity. It is not surrendering responsibility or abandoning intention. It is a different kind of participation—one that listens as much as it acts, that responds rather than controls. It is the willingness to take the step we can see, without demanding the entire road in advance.

In this posture, humility replaces urgency. We recognize that life is larger than our plans, that the soul carries wisdom beyond our timelines, and that mystery itself may be one of our greatest teachers. We begin to discover joy not only in arrival, but in movement itself—not only in answers, but in the unfolding of questions.

When we live this way, curiosity matures into reverence. The path is no longer a problem to solve or a destination to conquer. It becomes a sacred process—an ongoing conversation between who we are and who we are becoming. We are no longer rushing toward meaning. We are learning to walk with it.

And slowly, almost imperceptibly, something shifts.
We stop trying to force the journey forward.
We begin to allow it to carry us.

To let the path unfold is to recognize that seeking is not about reaching a finish line, but about learning how to walk with openness, trust, and wonder. In this way, the journey itself becomes sacred—not because it is clear, but because it is alive.

Closing Reflection

To walk with sacred curiosity is to loosen our grip on certainty and enter life as a living conversation. We begin to sense that the unknown is not something to overcome, but a space to honor. Rather than insisting that life conform to our timelines or expectations, we learn to move with the rhythm of unfolding—allowing each step to reveal what it carries, one moment at a time.

In this posture, something in us softens. Mystery is no longer resisted. Delay is no longer wasted time. Silence is no longer empty. We begin to recognize that the pauses, turns, and unanswered questions are not deviations from the journey, but part of its deeper intelligence. Curiosity teaches us to lean into wonder rather than fear, to remain open rather than guarded, to listen rather than rush.

Gradually, our understanding of the journey changes. We stop measuring life only by outcomes. Completion no longer defines meaning. Instead, the path itself becomes sacred—every question, every waiting, every subtle shift of awareness. The soul does not move in straight lines, but in spirals and seasons. What once felt like uncertainty begins to reveal itself as a deeper rhythm—one we cannot command, but can choose to enter.

Curiosity, in this light, is not a passing mood or idle wondering. It is a sacred posture—a willingness to meet life as it is, not only as we wish it to be. It steadies us when fear rises. It keeps us awake to grace in ordinary moments. It reminds us that we are always in dialogue with something larger, always being shaped by forces we do not fully see.

Yet curiosity is not the destination. It is the doorway.

For as much as life unfolds around us, something deeper has been awakening within us. What began as hunger has become listening. What began as longing has become direction. What began as seeking has quietly turned us inward.

And so the journey shifts.

What we once searched for beyond ourselves begins to reveal itself within. What felt like restlessness becomes recognition. What seemed distant begins to feel strangely familiar.

The path does not lead us away from ourselves.

It leads us home.

What began as hunger has become a listening.

And so the turning deepens…
revealing the light you have always carried.

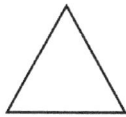

Part II - Finding: Remembering the Inner Source

The turning inward—
the light remembered within.

Chapter 5

The Treasure Within

What lies behind us and what lies before us are tiny matters
compared to what lies within us.
— Ralph Waldo Emerson

T here comes a moment when the outward search begins to soften. After so much effort, after wandering through the world for answers, a new awareness begins to dawn: what we have been longing for has always lived within us.

The treasure of the soul is not hidden in some distant realm, nor reserved for the rare, the perfected, or the chosen few. It has always been here—quietly present beneath the noise of proving, beneath the layers of fear, beneath the stories we have told ourselves about who we must be to belong. We do not earn this treasure, and we cannot lose it. It is the essence of who we are—whole, luminous, and held from within by the presence of the Divine.

This discovery rarely reveals itself all at once. More often, it dawns the way morning light does—gradually, almost imperceptibly at first. We notice it in small unveilings: a calm that rises in stillness, a deep exhale that follows surrender, a joy that appears naturally in a moment of genuine connection. These glimpses remind us that what we long for is not absent but woven into our being.

We do not have to pursue it. We remember it. We uncover what was never truly gone.

To find the treasure within is not to add something new to ourselves, but to awaken to what has always been present. What was never absent does not need retrieving—only recognition. The worth we crave, the belonging we yearn for, the love we have been reaching toward—none of these have ever been withheld at the deepest level. They live within us, waiting for us to turn and see.

This remembering changes everything. It reshapes how we walk through the world. Instead of living as if we must prove ourselves or complete ourselves, we begin to live from a deeper ground—the awareness that we already carry what we need. From this place, life becomes less about reaching outward for approval or accumulation, and more about embodying the truth we carry within.

The journey of seeking has prepared us for this. The hunger, the questions, the persistent searching—these were not mistakes. They were the soul's way of leading us here, to this turning point. The path of becoming is, at its heart, the path of remembrance. And what we are remembering now is the treasure within.

Across centuries and traditions, mystics have spoken of this treasure. Their voices echo across time, reminding us that what we seek is not far away but closer than our own breath.

This is the wisdom of the mystics: the indwelling Divine.

Mystics and the Indwelling Divine

When we turn inward and begin to sense the treasure within, we find ourselves in good company. Across cultures and centuries, mystics have named it in different ways—the spark of God, Divine Source, the kingdom within—yet all point toward the same reality: what we long for has been here all along.

The mystics insist that the spiritual journey is not a climb toward some far-off peak but an awakening to what is already present. Meister Eckhart spoke of a light in the soul that is "uncreated and uncreatable"—a radiance within us that cannot be manufactured or destroyed, because it belongs to the Divine itself.[1] Rumi pictured the soul as a dwelling where the Beloved is always present, even when we fail to recognize it.[2] The Upanishads whisper a startling truth—*Tat Tvam Asi*—("You are That") — pointing toward an inner identity that is not separate from the sacred ground of being.[3] Buddhist teachings speak of Buddha-nature, an innate capacity for awakening that remains

[1] Meister Eckhart, *The Essential Sermons, Commentaries, Treatises, and Defense*, translated by Edmund Colledge and Bernard McGinn (New York: Paulist Press, 1981), Sermon 9.

[2] Inspired by Rumi's poem *The Guest House* in *The Essential Rumi*, translated by Coleman Barks (San Francisco: HarperOne, 1995), 109–110.

[3] *Chandogya Upanishad* 6.8.7, in *The Upanishads*, translated by Eknath Easwaran (Tomales, CA: Nilgiri Press, 2007), 118.

untouched beneath confusion and conditioning.[4]

Different languages. Different symbols. One convergence: the Divine is not elsewhere. It is within.

This message is radical because it shifts the seat of authority. If the sacred is not found only in temples, rituals, or intermediaries, but in the heart of every soul, then no external system can claim to own it. Perhaps this is why mystics have often been resisted, dismissed, or muted. But their words endure because they do not function merely as doctrine—they resonate as recognition. Something in us knows what they are pointing toward.

Perhaps you have felt that recognition, too. A moment of stillness where peace rose freely, as though life itself were breathing through you. A flash of beauty that felt too vast to be only personal. A joy with no obvious cause, yet unmistakably real. These are not tricks of the mind. They are glimpses of the treasure—evidence that the indwelling presence has never left us, only waited to be remembered.

Mystics did not come to announce something new, but to confirm what has always been true. This treasure is not granted by external approval, nor diminished by our missteps. It is the essence of who we are—the sacred woven into every soul. Our work is not to create it but to uncover it—to allow what has been

---

[4] See the *Tathāgatagarbha Sūtra* and the *Mahāparinirvāṇa Sūtra*; see also Thich Nhat Hanh, *The Heart of the Buddha's Teaching* (New York: Broadway Books, 1998), pp. 49–50.

obscured by fear, distraction, or control to come forward again into light.

This truth does not separate us from the world. It roots us more deeply within it. For when we remember the Divine within, we begin to recognize the Divine everywhere—in ourselves, in others, and in the life that surrounds us.

The mystics across time have sung the same refrain: the kingdom is within you. Their voices echo now, urging us to pause, to turn inward, and to discover for ourselves what they have always known:

The treasure is already here.

Yet what is already here can still feel hidden.

That is the next turning of this chapter: learning to notice what has been with us all along.

The Hidden in Plain Sight

The truth is not that the treasure is absent, but that it is obscured. Not locked away in some unreachable place, but veiled beneath distraction, expectation, and forgetfulness. We have been trained to direct attention outward—toward achievement, possessions, relationships, approval—until the inner life becomes background noise. Like a jewel covered in dust, the radiance is not gone; it is simply unnoticed.

This is why mystics speak not of realization, but of uncovering—of brushing dust from a jewel that never lost its light. They remind us that the Divine does not enter from elsewhere to complete us. It has always been here—steady and luminous—like the sun behind clouds. What hides it is not absence, but inattention. What reveals it is not force, but remembrance.

Often, this remembrance does not come through dramatic revelations. More often, it emerges through the ordinary. The treasure shows itself in small, sacred moments: the hush of morning, the rise and fall of breath, the laughter of children, the steady beauty of the natural world, the unexpected kindness of another. These are not grand spectacles. They are gentle unveilings of Presence—woven into daily life, patiently awaiting recognition.

The sacred rarely announces itself with spectacle. More often, it appears in subtleties: a peace that settles without explanation, a stirring of love that surprises us, a clear inner knowing in a moment of silence. These moments can be so quiet we are tempted to dismiss them. Yet they are evidence of the treasure in plain sight.

Why does it reveal itself this way? Perhaps because recognition cannot be manufactured. Hiddenness slows us down. It draws us into attentiveness. It invites a different way of seeing—one that requires softness rather than urgency, listening rather than grasping.

In this sense, the hiddenness becomes a teacher. It transforms our restless reaching into receptive attention. It turns impatience into presence. It trains the inner senses, so that what has always been here can finally be perceived.

And when we do perceive it, the experience is not merely recognition—it is rediscovery.

The Joy of Rediscovery

There is a joy that comes not from adding to ourselves, but from rediscovering what was never truly lost. It is the intimate wonder of recognizing that what we searched for outside has been living within us all along.

This joy feels different from the brief satisfaction of accomplishment or novelty. It has the texture of relief and reverence. Relief, because we no longer have to exhaust ourselves in endless pursuit. Reverence, because it feels almost miraculous that something so steady, so sacred, so intimate has been waiting inside us—untouched by our forgetting.

Rediscovery feels sweet not because something was truly lost, but because forgetting made the remembering luminous. Like a familiar song suddenly recalled, or a beloved place revisited after years away, rediscovery carries tenderness and gratitude. It moves us not only because of what we have found, but because of what we now understand: the treasure never abandoned us. It was we who became distracted, hurried, or unaware.

This is why spiritual traditions speak of awakening and remembrance rather than attainment. We are not reaching a distant destination. We are waking up to what has always been true. We are returning home to a presence that has been faithfully within us since the beginning.

You may know this joy already: in a moment of stillness when peace rises for no reason; in a connection that opens the heart without effort; in a clarity that feels both personal and timeless. These are rediscoveries. These are reminders.

As rediscovery deepens, it changes how we see everything else. Once we glimpse the Divine within, we begin to recognize its reflection everywhere—shimmering in the faces of others, pulsing through the rhythms of nature, woven into the ordinary fabric of daily life. Rediscovery does not isolate us from the world; it reveals the sacredness saturating the world.

This is the great joy: not simply that we find, but that we remember. Not simply that we hold the treasure, but that we realize it has been holding us.

Rediscovery is homecoming. It is reunion. It is the soul whispering, *You were never separate. You were never incomplete. You were never alone.*

Closing Reflection

Mystics across time have pointed toward a truth both simple and radical: the Divine is not far away, but intimately near — dwelling at the center of our being. What we have sought with such longing has never been withheld. It has been here all along — steady as breath, quiet as heartbeat, hidden in plain sight.

Yet, hiddenness has its purpose. The treasure is not absent, but veiled — waiting for our pace to slow, our perception to soften, our attention to turn inward. This is why so many of us search outward first. We mistake the shimmer of externals for the gold of the soul. But when those externals reveal their limits, a deeper seeing becomes possible. What once seemed distant is revealed as the ground of who we are — the truth that was never elsewhere.

Rediscovery carries a joy unlike any other — not the fleeting satisfaction of pursuit, but the profound relief of remembering. The essence we thought we had to earn is already present. The belonging we thought we had to secure is already rooted within. The love we thought we had to chase is already woven into our being.

This remembering changes how we move through life. We no longer live as if we must prove our worth or manufacture wholeness. We begin to live from the inner source. And as we do, the world itself begins to look different — not because it has changed, but because we are seeing with new eyes.

The treasure within has been recognized. Now the journey turns toward its reflection: how the world mirrors back what is awakening inside us—how life itself becomes a sacred display of what we have begun to remember.

The treasure within has been found.
Now we learn to see it everywhere.

Chapter 6

The Mirror of Creation

Your vision will become clear only when you can look into your own heart.
Who looks outside, dreams; who looks inside, awakes.
— Carl Jung

When we begin to awaken to the treasure within, something subtle yet profound shifts in how we perceive the world. Life no longer appears as a series of disconnected events. Instead, it begins to reveal itself as a mirror—reflecting the inner patterns, beliefs, and longings that shape our experience. Encounters, moments of joy, and moments of challenge all become part of this sacred reflection, inviting us into deeper self-recognition.

This is not a doctrine of blame, nor a simplistic formula that reduces life to cause and effect. The mirror of creation is more spacious and compassionate. It does not accuse; it reveals. It does not assign fault; it illuminates resonance. Through it, we begin to notice where our inner life is aligned and where it is seeking restoration. The mirror is not a judge. It is a teacher.

To live with this awareness is to notice meaning where we once saw only circumstance. Conflict, for example, is not always confined to the present moment. It may stir something older— a tender pattern within us that has long awaited recognition.

What rises in moments of tension is often not an attack, but an invitation to awareness and integration.

A disappointment may reveal an attachment that no longer reflects who we are becoming. A moment of beauty may awaken us to the love already alive within. The mirror reflects not to diminish us, but to call us toward truth — and truth, when welcomed, becomes a doorway into freedom.

At first, this perspective can feel unsettling. We may resist what the mirror reveals, especially when the reflection challenges familiar narratives. Yet over time, we begin to sense that even difficult images are not judgments, but invitations. Each reflection carries the possibility of deeper alignment and a more authentic way of being.

The mirror of creation is not here to overwhelm us. It reminds us that inner and outer are always in conversation. Our thoughts, emotions, and beliefs color how we perceive the world, and the world, in turn, reflects what we carry within. To notice this dialogue is to step into a more conscious participation in life. We become both learners and creators — receiving insight from experience while shaping what is reflected through inner awareness.

When we recognize this mirror, we begin to understand that the treasure within is not meant to remain hidden. It shines outward, reflected back through people, circumstances, and the unfolding rhythms of our days. Life becomes a living mirror, continually guiding us toward who we are and who we are becoming.

To walk with this awareness changes how we meet experience. Challenges are no longer interpreted as verdicts against us or evidence that we are lacking, but as reflections—signals that reveal, orient, and guide. The mirror of creation does not judge us; it invites us into deeper truth, so that we may live more fully from the treasure within.

This is where the journey now turns: learning to see life as reflection rather than judgment.

Life as Reflection, Not Judgment

When we first encounter the idea that life mirrors us, it can stir discomfort. Many of us carry inherited beliefs about reward and consequence, and it is easy to assume that challenge means something has gone wrong. We may imagine the universe as a strict arbiter, assigning experiences as judgments about our worth. But this is not the nature of the mirror.

Life does not operate as a system of retribution. The mirror of creation does not operate as a moral ledger or a measure of worth. It simply reflects. Just as a physical mirror shows what stands before it without commentary, life reflects the inner landscapes of belief, feeling, and perception. It does not say, *You are wrong*. It says, *This is what is present*.

This distinction is essential. To interpret life as judgment breeds fear and contraction. To interpret life as reflection opens a pathway to learning, compassion, and transformation. The mirror is not here to diminish us; it is here to awaken us.

When we carry fear, life often reveals it—not to diminish us, but to bring it into awareness so it can be transformed. When we carry love, life reflects it back, expanding its presence in our experience. When unintegrated stories linger within us, situations arise that bring them to light, inviting recognition and wholeness. These are not sentences imposed by an external authority. They are invitations to coherence.

This does not mean we control every event or circumstance. Life is vast, shaped by collective forces, natural rhythms, and the choices of others. Yet within this vastness, the mirror reveals how our inner orientation shapes how we experience and respond. It reflects resonance, not domination.

When we release the idea of retribution, something in us softens. We become less defensive, less afraid of what life brings. Even challenging experiences begin take on a different texture—not as proof of misalignment, but as invitations to insight and choice. A closed door becomes a redirection. A conflict becomes a call to awareness. A season of emptiness becomes an opening to root in what endures.

The mirror is not distant. It is intimate. It meets us exactly where we are, revealing what is ready to be seen. And when we shift our question from *Why is this happening to me?* to *What is being revealed through this?*, we move from fear into freedom.

Life as reflection draws us into dialogue with reality itself. Instead of bracing against experience, we begin to listen to it. We stop interpreting life as a verdict against us and begin engaging it as conversation.

Here the mirror reveals its deeper wisdom: reflection is not one-sided. Our inner life and outer experience are woven together in a living exchange.

This is the next step—to recognize the dialogue between thought, feeling, and reality.

The Dialogue of Thought, Feeling, Reality

When we begin to see life as reflection, a deeper pattern emerges: inner and outer are not separate. Thought, feeling, and experience are woven into an ongoing dialogue.

Every thought carries orientation. Thoughts shaped by scarcity or self-doubt narrow perception, limiting what we believe is possible. When we hold such thoughts, we often act in ways that confirm them. If we believe our voice does not matter, we may silence ourselves—and in doing so, encounter the very invisibility we feared.

Conversely, thoughts shaped by openness expand perception. They change how we enter rooms, how we interpret encounters, how we recognize possibility. A person who trusts in connection is more likely to notice it, welcome it, and reflect it back. Thought does not dictate reality, but it prepares the field in which experience unfolds.

Feelings deepen this dialogue. Emotions are not passive states; they shape presence. Fear contracts; openness expands. When we ignore inner signals, they do not disappear—they reappear in new forms, seeking recognition. When we listen, they become sources of clarity and direction.

Life responds within this exchange. Experience shapes thought and feeling, which then shape the next experience. Over time, patterns form. Unexamined beliefs repeat themselves. Unacknowledged emotions surface again, not as judgment, but as invitation.

Awareness transforms this cycle. When we notice the dialogue, we gain choice. We can pause, soften, and reorient. In that moment, the pattern shifts. A cycle of contraction can give way to spaciousness. A story of limitation can open into possibility.

This dialogue is not about controlling life or forcing outcomes. It is about conscious participation. We are neither powerless nor omnipotent. We are participants in a living exchange—shaping and being shaped, reflecting and being reflected.

As this awareness deepens, our vision changes. The world may not change overnight, but our perception does.
We begin to see with new eyes.

Seeing With New Eyes

Awareness reshapes vision. When we recognize the dialogue between inner life and outer experience, the world does not suddenly transform—but our way of seeing does. Events that once felt random begin to reveal coherence. What seemed disconnected begins to feel conversational.

Seeing with new eyes is not a refusal of what is difficult. It is a shift in orientation. Instead of interpreting experiences as final verdicts, we begin to perceive them as reflections. Instead of collapsing into reaction, we turn toward inquiry. In this shift, even ordinary moments become openings.

With new eyes, experiences become layered with meaning. A disagreement reveals the need for boundaries or deeper understanding. A disappointment reveals attachments ready to be released. Moments of beauty become reminders of the presence already alive within.

This way of seeing also softens our relationship with difficulty. Instead of interpreting challenge as judgment, we begin to recognize it as revelation—a signal that something within us is ready for integration. The experience does not lose its intensity, but it gains context.

At the same time, wonder expands. The ordinary becomes luminous. Breath becomes reminder. Stillness becomes presence. Connection becomes echo. With new eyes, life appears saturated with meaning—not because it has changed, but because we have become attentive.

To see in this way is not to withdraw from life, but to enter it more fully. The mirror does not spare us from complexity, but it transforms how we meet it. What once felt random begins to reveal coherence. What once felt adversarial becomes instructive.

Seeing with new eyes is not escape; it is participation. It is the recognition that we are always living within a mirror—one that reveals, refines, and guides us back to the treasure within.

Closing Reflection

Life is a mirror, reflecting us not in judgment, but in revelation. It shows the patterns we carry, the beliefs that shape us, the feelings that quietly influence our choices. It reflects the love we have embraced and the parts of ourselves still waiting to be integrated.

To recognize this mirror is to step into dialogue with existence itself. Thought, feeling, and experience move together in a living exchange. When fear dominates, life reflects contraction. When openness emerges, life reflects possibility. The mirror does not coerce; it responds.

Seeing with new eyes becomes a turning point. Instead of resisting what appears, we begin to listen. Experiences are no longer verdicts, but messages. Beauty becomes recognition.

Silence becomes presence. Difficulty becomes invitation. In this way, life reveals both light and shadow—not to divide us, but to draw us toward wholeness. The mirror does not ask us to choose one over the other. It invites us to integrate both.

This chapter does not close with certainty, but with readiness. Having recognized the mirror, we are prepared for its deeper work: not merely to see our reflections, but to gather them into unity.

The treasure within has been remembered.
The mirror of creation has revealed its language.
Now the journey moves toward integration—
where reflection becomes embodiment, and awareness
becomes wholeness.

Chapter 7

Integrating Light and Shadow

Wholeness is not achieved by cutting off a portion of one's being,
but by integration of the contraries.
— *Carl Jung*

When we first awaken to the treasure within, the experience can feel like sunlight breaking through clouds—warm, radiant, affirming. We may imagine the path ahead as ever-increasing light, as though the work of the soul is to transcend all darkness and live only in clarity and peace.

But soon, the mirror of creation begins to reflect back more than our brilliance. It reveals the hidden places too: the shadow we carry, the tender memories we tucked away, the parts of ourselves we tried to outgrow or forget.

This can feel disorienting. We may wonder if we've taken a wrong turn—if this unveiling means we are moving backward rather than forward. Yet the truth is quite the opposite. Meeting the shadow is not a detour away from wholeness; it is the next necessary movement toward it. Awakening does not bypass the shadow—it brings it into view. The light within us is not meant to erase what is difficult, but to meet it with presence and gather it into a larger belonging.

The shadow is not our enemy. It is simply the name we give to what has gone unacknowledged: the anger we feared, the grief we muted, the longings we dismissed, the truths we didn't yet know how to hold. These fragments often wait with a subtle patience, surfacing when we are ready to see them. They appear in reflections that unsettle us: the patterns that repeat, the emotions that flare unexpectedly, the inner stories that whisper we are not enough. These are not signs that something has gone wrong. They are signs that something deeper is asking to be recognized.

Integration is the practice of welcoming these fragments home. It is not about perfecting ourselves or purifying what we dislike. It is remembering that the Divine indwells the whole of who we are—not just the polished or socially acceptable parts. To integrate shadow and light is to look with gentler eyes at our complexity and to discover, with time, how what once seemed troubling can become meaningful when held in awareness.

Fear can become steadiness when met honestly.
Grief can deepen compassion when honored.
Anger can reveal clarity when understood.

What we once turned away from begins to speak differently when we stop resisting it. The very parts we rejected often carry gifts hidden beneath their rough edges. A tender place we avoided can open the way to greater compassion. A misstep can become the soil of discernment. Even anger, when listened to, may reveal the boundary that protects what is sacred.

What once felt like a weight, when welcomed, becomes a teacher. The rejected part softens—not because it was "fixed," but because it was finally included. In that inclusion, what was once exile becomes offering.

The soul does not hunger for perfection; it longs for wholeness. And wholeness requires that nothing be left outside the field of love. Light without shadow can become denial. Shadow without light can become despair. But when the two are held together, we begin to live in a truer kind of freedom—one that does not deny our history, but transforms it into wisdom.

This chapter invites us into that work: not erasing, not correcting, not forcing ourselves into an impossible purity—but the sacred work of reunion. For to integrate shadow and light is to step into the fullness of our being and recognize that even the hidden corners are touched by the treasure within.

To begin this work, we turn toward the very parts of ourselves we have tried hardest to avoid. The shadow is often made of fragments—memories, emotions, desires—that at some point we decided were too heavy, too shameful, or too much to carry.

But they are still with us. And the first step of integration is simple: to notice them, to name them, and to welcome them back into belonging.

This is where we begin: with the pieces we once rejected.

The Pieces We Once Rejected

Every soul carries pieces it has tried to cast away. Some we buried so early that we barely remember they exist. Others we learned, over time, to hide more carefully. These are the parts of us that once felt too disruptive, too overwhelming, or too unwelcome to remain in the light of acceptance.

It may have been anger—rising naturally to protect us—but quickly silenced by those who told us we were "too much." It may have been grief—wanting to be felt—yet hurried along by a world that prizes composure. It may have been tenderness— the part that longed for safety and closeness—closed down after betrayal or loss.

Vulnerability, desire, creativity, even joy itself: any of these can be exiled into shadow when life convinces us they are not safe to carry openly.

Over time, we build identities around what seems acceptable. We highlight our strengths, refine our outer image, and learn to perform the version of ourselves most likely to be approved. Yet beneath the surface, the rejected pieces remain. They do not vanish simply because we deny them. They linger, shaping us beneath awareness, surfacing in ways we cannot fully direct.

Suppressed anger can leak out sideways as irritation, cynicism, or self-criticism. Unmet grief can harden into numbness, muting both sorrow and joy.

Exiled tenderness can become defensiveness,
closing the door to intimacy.

In truth, what we reject does not disappear; it waits. It waits for us to turn toward it with enough courage, enough love, to say, *I see you. You belong.*

This is why life keeps bringing us back to these hidden places. The mirror of creation reflects them through repeating patterns, difficult relationships, or emotions that rise when we least expect them. These are not judgments. They are invitations — reminders that what we cast aside is still part of the whole.

To turn toward these pieces is one of the bravest movements of the soul. It asks us to release judgment and meet what we once feared. When we do, something softens. We begin to see that these fragments were never here to ruin us. They carry wisdom:

- anger that clarifies boundaries
- grief that deepens love
- vulnerability that opens intimacy
- creativity that restores aliveness

Integration begins with recognition: pausing long enough to notice the part of us that feels unwanted and whispering, *You matter. You are welcome here.*

This does not mean acting out every emotion or indulging every impulse. It means giving these pieces a seat at the table of our being — honoring their message, letting them be heard, and discovering the deeper truth they hold.

Slowly, gently, we gather ourselves back together—
not as flawless beings, but as whole ones.

This is where the deeper truth of integration emerges: wholeness is not found by polishing away the shadow, but by including it.

To live whole is to welcome all of ourselves into the circle of love.

Wholeness as Inclusion

We are often taught to equate wholeness with perfection. From childhood onward, subtle messages suggest that to be whole is to be flawless—free of contradiction, untouched by uncertainty, always composed. In that framing, wholeness becomes a distant standard: something we try to reach, yet rarely feel we embody.

But true wholeness is not found in flawlessness.
It is found in inclusion.

The soul's invitation is not to cut away what we dislike or deny what we fear. It is to welcome everything we are—the strong and the tender, the confident and the uncertain, the radiant and the hidden.

Anger can point to what we value and where our boundaries are asking to be honored.

Grief can deepen our capacity to love.

Fear can teach us presence, discernment, and steadiness. Shame, when met with gentleness, can reveal the longing beneath it: the longing to belong and be seen as worthy.

Inclusion does not mean surrendering to every impulse. It means allowing what arises to be seen, so it can take its rightful place in the larger harmony of who we are. When denied, these parts often influence us from below the surface. When welcomed, they soften and integrate.

When we live in exclusion—cutting off parts of ourselves—we become divided. One side reaches for approval while another hides in fear of exposure. That division drains us. But when we live in inclusion, something different takes root: we become grounded, honest, and more at ease in our own skin.

Wholeness as inclusion is, at its heart, a practice of compassion. It is treating yourself as you would treat someone you love— not as a project to perfect, but as a being to hold.

When we choose inclusion, we begin to discover beauty in what we once labeled a defect. Our cracks let light through. Our struggles deepen our humanity. Our contradictions reveal our depth.

Wholeness is not the absence of shadow, but the embrace of both shadow and light. It is the courage to say:

Every part of me belongs.
Every part of me is worthy of being seen.
Every part of me is held in love.

Here is the surprising grace: when we release the demand for perfection and include the whole of who we are, what we once hid begins to reveal its unassuming beauty.

Not the beauty of being finished—but the beauty of being real.

The Beauty of the Unpolished

We are taught, often without realizing it, to associate beauty with refinement. We learn that what is smooth is preferable to what is rough; what is controlled feels safer than what is unguarded; what appears "complete" is more acceptable than what is still becoming.

Over time, this teaching turns inward.

So we learn to polish.
We soften what feels too sharp.
We hide what feels unfinished.
We edit what might make others uncomfortable.

We become careful about which parts of ourselves we display and which we keep tucked away: the tremble in our voice, the sensitivity we never outgrew, the questions that refuse easy answers, the memories that still shape us.

Slowly, we refine our image until the version we present feels safer—yet sometimes less true.

Yet something vital is often lost in this polishing.

Because the soul does not crave perfection. It craves authenticity—and authenticity is rarely seamless. It carries the marks of being lived. It holds the imprint of what shaped us.

The unpolished places—the ones we most want to correct or conceal—are often the most honest. They are where life entered us most deeply, where we were changed, softened, humbled, awakened.

Our rough edges are not deformities.
They are evidence.

Evidence that we have lived.
Evidence that we have been touched by love and loss.
Evidence that life has shaped us rather than passed us by.

The unpolished places are not signs that something has gone wrong. They are signs of passage. They remind us that transformation is rarely neat, that growth is not a straight line, that becoming whole is less about smoothing everything out and more about allowing all of it to belong.

An unpolished soul is not a careless one.
It is often a courageous one.

It belongs to someone loosening their grip on appearances—someone no longer trying so hard to look "finished," because they have begun to understand that wholeness is not a perfected state. It is a spacious one.

To live unpolished does not mean rejecting growth. It means changing our relationship with it. Moving away from relentless self-correction and into deeper self-recognition. Allowing the unfinished places to breathe without immediately trying to alter them.

Because it is often in what remains unrefined that the deepest truth reveals itself.

The tremor in our voice can speak of sincerity.
The tear we could not hold back can speak of tenderness.
The doubt we carry can speak of humility.

These are not defects. They are the texture of a life lived with feeling.

Perhaps this is the deeper beauty:
not the beauty of perfection, but the beauty of presence.
not the beauty of control, but the beauty of truth.

Wholeness is not discovered by polishing away our humanity. It is discovered by including it. In that inclusion, what we once tried to smooth over becomes a threshold—not because it is broken, but because it is real.

Closing Reflection

Integration is the art of remembering that nothing within us is disposable. The pieces we once rejected—anger we buried, grief we silenced, tenderness we hid, longings we feared—carry threads of wisdom waiting to be woven back into the fabric of our being. They are not detours from wholeness; they are part of how wholeness is formed.

Wholeness is not born from polishing away inner tension or silencing unease. It emerges through the courageous inclusion of everything we are. Not through flawlessness, but through saying yes to the full spectrum of our being. In gathering the fragments, the hidden places, and allowing them to stand in the light of love, we discover a strength perfection can never offer: the strength of authenticity.

As we practice inclusion, something begins to change. What once felt like an unintegrated place starts to reveal its unexpected beauty. The openings we once tried to conceal become places where light can enter. The marks life has etched into us become signs of resilience and depth. The unpolished places—tender and honest—carry a radiance no mask of composure can replicate.

This is the paradox of the soul: the places we thought disqualified us are often the places where grace becomes most visible. Shadow is not a threat, but invitation. When held with compassion, it becomes teacher. When met with presence, what was once avoided becomes a threshold into wisdom.

Integration is not about arriving at a final state where nothing stirs. It is learning to live with yourself in honesty and tenderness, moment by moment. Wholeness is not static; it is living inclusion. It is the practice of coming home again and again, in all your complexity.

This is why integration naturally leads us toward presence. To live whole, we learn to stay with what is—neither fleeing the shadow nor clinging to the light, but being here for both.

Presence becomes the ground where integration continues: the steady practice that holds together all we are discovering.

So the path turns once more. Having gathered what was exiled, and welcomed the unpolished into love, we now step into the rhythm that sustains it all: the discipline of presence.

Chapter 8

The Discipline of Presence

The only true paradise is the paradise of presence.
— Bert McCoy

Integration gathers us, but presence sustains us. To welcome shadow and light is not a single moment—it is an ongoing way of living. And the thread that makes it possible is presence. Without presence, the soul's invitations move right past us. Without presence, we are carried by distraction, judgment, and the old habits of fragmentation. Presence is the ground where healing becomes lived reality.

Presence is not the same as stillness, though it often brings calm. Nor is it an escape into silence or a detachment from life. Presence is active rather than passive: a choice to remain awake and available to the moment we are in—to the breath, the body, the inner currents, and the life moving around us. It is the willingness to let things be as they are long enough to hear what they are revealing.

This discipline matters because the mind is a wandering traveler. It darts forward into anticipation, backward into memory, sideways into comparison. The mind is rarely here. But the soul? The soul only ever dwells in the present. When we return to presence, we align ourselves with the rhythm of the soul. We remember that life is not something we will someday live once we are prepared, accomplished, or "ready."

Life is happening now, and presence is how we meet it.

Presence is also what transforms awareness into integration. It is one thing to believe, in theory, that all parts of us belong. It is another to remain with the heat of anger without pushing it away, to breathe with the weight of grief without numbing, to honor the flicker of joy without dismissing it as small. Without presence, we bypass or overlook. With presence, we stay. We feel. We welcome. We integrate.

This practice is not about achieving a perfect, unshakable calm. Presence is not measured by how rarely we drift, but by how gently—and how often—we return. Each return is a homecoming: to breath, to body, to the truth of who we are. Each return is an act of remembering: remembering the treasure within, remembering that every moment carries the possibility of awakening.

Presence does not remove us from ordinary life; it transforms it. The discipline of presence belongs not only to meditation or prayer, but to the whole of life: the drive to work and the line at the market, the arguments and the laughter, the fatigue and the wonder. Presence allows us to show up with greater clarity, depth, and authenticity in every corner of our days.

To live this way is to let life itself become a practice ground. Each moment offers a chance to return. Each breath becomes an invitation to awaken. Each encounter becomes a mirror of the soul's wholeness. Presence gathers us, centers us, and becomes the soil from which conscious creation can grow.

If presence is the ground, attention is the way we step onto it. Attention is how presence begins—the simple, courageous act of noticing. When we turn the gaze of awareness toward what is here, even briefly, we discover that the doorway to presence is always open.

So we begin with attention: the doorway into presence.

Attention as Doorway

Presence may sound like a lofty spiritual ideal, but in lived experience it begins with something simple, tender, and always available: attention. Attention is the way we enter the present moment. It is the doorway, the gentle turning of awareness toward what is already here.

Many of us confuse attention with focus, but they are not the same. Focus is narrow and directive, like a beam trained on a single point. Attention, in its deeper sense, is spacious and receptive. It does not strain or demand; it allows. Attention is like opening a window—suddenly the air moves, light enters, and we sense the aliveness we had overlooked. It is a soft but steady gaze that honors what is present, whether ordinary or extraordinary.

This shift may seem subtle, yet it changes everything. When we offer attention to the breath, we return to our center. When we notice the sensations of the body, we come home to our own ground. When we listen deeply—to a bird's call, to a friend's voice, to the quiet stirrings of the heart—presence begins to take root. Attention slows the rushing mind, softens the guarded heart, and opens the body to inhabit the moment.

The beauty of this doorway is its nearness. We do not need special conditions or elaborate rituals to enter it. Presence is not reserved for retreats or silent rooms. It is as close as the next breath, as ordinary as warm water on the hands, as immediate as noticing sunlight on the skin. Attention transforms daily life into sacred ground.

Attention is also an act of self-compassion. It is how we begin to welcome all of ourselves without judgment. When anger arises, we can notice its heat without suppressing it. When grief surfaces, we can feel its weight without turning away. When joy appears, we can linger with it without diminishing it. Attention does not rush or restrain; it simply says, I am here with this. And in that space of presence, transformation begins.

Of course, attention drifts. The mind wanders forward into anticipation and backward into memory. This drifting is not a failure of practice; it is the nature of the mind. The practice is not to remain perfectly attentive, but to notice when we have wandered and gently return. Every act of noticing is itself attention. Every return is already presence.

Attention is not a doorway we pass through once. It is a doorway we return to again and again. Presence is sustained not by a single moment of awareness, but by the rhythm of returning.

So the practice deepens: learning to come back.

Returning Again and Again

Presence is not a state we achieve and maintain without drift. It is a rhythm, a practice of returning. Inevitably, the mind will wander, the heart will tighten, the body will brace. We will be swept into distraction—pulled by fear, carried by habit, absorbed in stories of past and future. This is not evidence of something wrong. It is simply the texture of being human.

The gift is that presence is never truly lost. It waits, patient and steady, in every moment. The instant we realize we have drifted, we are already at the threshold of return. Each breath invites us back. Each pause opens space. Each noticing— even the awareness of being far away—is already a form of presence.

This rhythm of wandering and returning weaves presence into the fabric of our lives. It is not the absence of drifting, but the willingness to return that transforms us. Over time, the return becomes less effortful, more natural. Instead of pulling ourselves back with harshness, we begin to soften. We smile at our wandering. We welcome ourselves home with kindness. We learn that presence is not fragile, not easily broken. It is wide enough to include even our forgetting.

As this rhythm takes root, something subtle shifts within us. We become less reactive, less swept by every wave of circumstance. We know that storms will come, but we also know how to find our footing again. We stop expecting ourselves to live in constant clarity and begin to trust the flow: drift and return, forget and remember, close and open. Each cycle strengthens us—not by preventing us from stumbling, but by teaching us how to rise with grace.

Returning again and again is how presence moves from insight into lived reality. It is how presence enters the ordinary acts of living—the way we listen, the way we breathe through tension, the way we pause to notice a moment of beauty. Each return, however small, roots us more deeply in reality. And in those rooted moments, even the ordinary begins to glow with meaning.

You do not need to master unbroken awareness. You need only be willing to return.

Presence is not about never leaving.
Presence is about always coming back.

In this rhythm of return, something unexpected begins to grow within us: a settled steadiness that does not depend on perfection, but on presence itself.

The Quiet Strength of Being Here

There is a strength that does not seek recognition, does not rush, and does not demand the world's approval. It is not the strength of constant activity, relentless productivity, or rigid control. It is quieter, subtler, and yet far more enduring. It is the strength that arises from simply being here.

As we practice returning, presence begins to weave itself into the fabric of our lives. At first, it appears in brief moments—a breath, a pause, a flicker of awareness easily lost. But over time, these moments become threads of steadiness, weaving into a tapestry that holds us even when everything else shifts. Presence teaches us that strength is not always resistance. Often, it is rootedness.

Like a tree whose branches sway while its roots reach deep into the soil, presence anchors us when life becomes turbulent. It does not shield us from difficulty, but it changes how we meet it. We still feel grief, fear, tenderness, and longing—but we discover a center within us that remains steady. Presence does not remove the storm; it gives us ground within it.

There is steady courage in choosing to stay when everything in us wants to escape. To remain with grief instead of numbing it. To notice fear instead of being ruled by it. To welcome joy without bracing for its disappearance. These are not small acts. They are expressions of inner maturity—the willingness to meet life as it is, without abandoning ourselves.

Over time, this strength reshapes how we live. We rely less on external markers of stability—approval, achievement, control—and more on the groundedness presence offers within. We learn that we do not need certainty in order to walk forward. We do not need to resolve everything before we can rest. We discover that even uncertainty can be held when we are anchored in presence.

Unlike the brittle strength of control, the quiet strength of presence is gentle. It does not harden us against life; it softens us into it. It allows us to open to beauty without fear, to vulnerability without collapse, to mystery without panic. It is not a strength we manufacture. It is a strength that arises when we allow ourselves to be fully here.

To be here is to discover strength in its most human and soul-deep form. It is to stand rooted in presence, trusting that whatever the moment brings, we have within us the steadiness to meet it—not by conquering it, but by inhabiting it.

Closing Reflection

Presence is the quiet thread weaving through every step of the journey. It begins with attention—the simple turning toward what is here. It deepens through returning—the gentle rhythm of coming back when we drift. And as it settles into our lives, presence reveals itself as a quiet strength: a rooted steadiness that grows not from control, but from the willingness to remain.

This strength is unlike the world's versions of strength. It does not seek validation or display. It endures quietly. It is not the strength of perfection or productivity, but the strength of staying with what is real. It allows us to breathe through grief, meet fear without surrendering to it, and receive joy without diminishing it. It is not loud, but it is unwavering.

Presence does not eliminate life's storms, but it anchors us so we are not swept away. Like roots reaching deep beneath shifting soil, presence grounds us in the soul. Difficulty may arise, uncertainty may linger, but the center holds. To be present is not to be untouched by life — it is to discover that even in life's intensity, we are held.

Over time, presence transforms how we walk through the world. We stop looking outside ourselves for stability and begin to trust the groundedness within. We realize that life does not need to be mastered to be lived. We do not need full clarity in order to take the next step. We do not need to erase our shadows in order to stand in the light. Presence teaches us to belong to ourselves in every season.

In this way, presence sanctifies the ordinary. The smallest moments—a pause between words, the hush before sleep, the warmth of morning light—become thresholds of wonder. Life begins to shimmer, not because it has changed, but because we have begun to see.

Yet presence is not an ending. It is the ground from which the next movement of the journey arises. From presence flows alignment. From wholeness flows expression. From rootedness flows the capacity to create consciously.

So the path turns once more. What has been sought and found within now asks to be lived outwardly—embodied, expressed, and offered as life. With presence as anchor and wholeness as center, we step into the rhythm of creation.

And so the journey moves from remembering who we are to learning how to live from what we have remembered.

What was sought outside was revealed as what had always lived within.

And so truth takes form...
choosing to live through you.

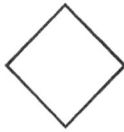

Part III - Being: Living as Conscious Creator

The grounding—
the truth lived in thought, word, and deed.

Chapter 9

The Power of Alignment

Alignment is when thought, word, and deed speak the same truth.
— Kea Rivers

Creation is not the privilege of a few; it is the nature of being human. We create not only through art or innovation, but through the subtle architecture of daily life. With every thought we hold, every word we speak, every choice we embody, we shape the field of our experience. Our lives are not static realities; they are unfolding expressions.

The question is not whether we are creators, but whether we are conscious of what we are creating—and whether what we create reflects the truth of who we are.

Presence anchors us in being.
Alignment carries that being into expression.

When thought, word, and deed move together, life begins to feel coherent rather than scattered. Something subtle shifts: the inner division softens, the tension between who we feel ourselves to be and how we live begins to dissolve. We are no longer pulled in opposing directions. Instead, we experience a living unity—a resonance between inner truth and outer form.

This is the power of alignment. Not control, not domination of outcomes, but coherence of being.

Alignment is not perfection. It is not the absence of fragmentation or uncertainty. It is the willingness to notice when we drift and to return, again and again, to what feels most true. Each return deepens trust in the inner compass. Over time, alignment becomes less effortful and more natural—like a river finding its course, like breath settling into rhythm.

When we live aligned, life changes its texture. Decisions become clearer, not because they are easier, but because they are rooted in coherence. Challenges remain, but they no longer fragment us. Tension becomes a place to practice truth rather than abandon it. Creation ceases to feel strained; it becomes expression.

To understand alignment, we must begin where creation itself begins: in the harmony of thought, word, and deed.

Harmony of Thought, Word, and Deed

Alignment is not an abstract ideal. It is lived in the relationship between what we think, what we say, and what we do. These three currents form the architecture of creation.

Thought is the seed.
It shapes the field of possibility before anything takes form.

When thought is rooted in scarcity or fear, it narrows perception and constricts choice. When thought arises from remembrance, trust, and truth, it opens space for new forms of life to emerge. Thought does not dictate reality, but it prepares the ground in which reality unfolds.

Word is the bridge.
It carries thought from the invisible into the shared world.

Words are not neutral. They declare, affirm, and shape meaning. When our words echo what we truly believe, they strengthen coherence. When our words contradict our inner knowing, a subtle fracture forms. Something in us recognizes the dissonance even when others do not.

Deed is the embodiment.
It is where truth becomes visible.

Action gives weight to thought and word. When what we do reflects what we know and what we say, integrity takes root. When our actions diverge from our inner truth, the body registers the division. Alignment is felt not only in the mind, but in the nervous system, in the breath, in the sense of ease or contraction that accompanies our choices.

When thought, word, and deed move together, life feels unified. We no longer edit ourselves for belonging or dilute our truth for approval. We trust ourselves because our inner and outer lives speak the same language.

When word and inner truth diverge, fragmentation emerges.

Energy drains not from circumstance alone, but from the effort of holding who we are inwardly and who we present outwardly in tension. Yet this fragmentation is not judgment; it is information. Each moment of awareness becomes an invitation to return.

Alignment is not achieved once. It is practiced continuously. Each return deepens coherence. Each act of honesty strengthens the current. Over time, alignment begins to feel less like discipline and more like freedom.

From this freedom, resonance emerges.

When Life Flows in Resonance

There are moments when life seems to move with us rather than against us. Not because friction disappears, but because something within us has settled into harmony. Thought, word, and deed no longer pull apart; they rise together. In that unity, we feel resonance.

Resonance is not perfection.
It is coherence.

In resonance, challenges still arise, but they no longer destabilize identity. Instead of reacting from fragmentation, we respond from wholeness. The energy once consumed by inner conflict becomes available for presence, creativity, and discernment.

Resonance clarifies. Choices feel less tangled. Direction feels less forced. We begin to sense, often in the body, what expands and what contracts, what feels aligned and what feels hollow. Life becomes a mirror not only of circumstance, but of coherence. The outer world reflects the quality of our inner alignment—not as judgment, but as resonance.

Resonance also carries an unforced magnetism.
Coherence awakens recognition.

Others feel it, even if they cannot name it. Some are drawn toward it. Others resist it. Either way, alignment becomes visible. Resonance cannot be manufactured; it emerges naturally when inner truth is lived outwardly.

When coherence takes root within, it begins to express itself without.

From resonance emerges a deeper gift: congruence.

The Ease of Congruence

Congruence is the experience of living without inner contradiction. It does not eliminate difficulty; it dissolves division.

Much of what exhausts us is not the weight of life itself, but the weight of living against ourselves. To believe one thing while acting another, to speak words that do not reflect our knowing, to silence what feels true—this quiet division erodes vitality.

Congruence releases that erosion.

When the inner compass and outer choices align, energy is no longer wasted. Life feels lighter not because it is easier, but because it is honest. Masks fall away. Pretending becomes unnecessary. Even when the path is steep, we carry less burden because we are no longer carrying inner division.

Congruence clarifies choice.

Instead of countless competing voices, a single question emerges: Does this reflect who I am becoming?

The answer may require courage, but it rarely lacks clarity. With clarity comes ease—not the ease of avoidance, but the ease of integrity.

Congruence deepens trust.

Each aligned choice strengthens the relationship with the self. We learn that we do not need certainty to move forward; we need coherence. Even sacrifice, when rooted in truth, carries dignity rather than depletion.

To live congruently is not to live flawlessly. It is to live whole. In that wholeness, creation ceases to be effortful. It becomes expression. Life begins to feel less like something to manage and more like something to embody.

This is the quiet power of alignment.

Closing Reflection

Alignment is the art of coherence. It begins where thought, word, and deed learn to move together—not in perfection, but in honesty. From that honesty emerges resonance, the inner hum that signals we are no longer divided against ourselves. From resonance arises congruence, the ease of living without disguise.

This is not the power of control.
It is the power of coherence.

When we are aligned, creation shifts in nature. It is no longer driven by urgency or fear, but by embodiment. Life begins to mirror not what we demand, but what we are. Reality responds less to effort and more to frequency—the quality of being we inhabit.

Alignment, then, is not merely personal integrity.
It is the threshold of conscious creation.

Here the question changes.
Not, What must I make happen?
But, What must I embody?
Not, How can I control life?
But, How can I attune myself to the truth I wish to live?

So the path turns again.
Having learned coherence, we are invited into a deeper dimension of creation—not as architects of outcomes, but as

stewards of frequency. From alignment we move into attunement, from coherence into vibration, from doing into being.

Creation now becomes subtler, steadier, and more powerful.

And so we step forward—
from alignment into the dance of frequency,
from coherence into conscious creation.

Chapter 10

Choosing Frequencies, Not Outcomes

Life responds to the frequency we embody.
— Kea Rivers

From the time we are young, we are taught to measure life in outcomes. Grades, milestones, promotions, and achievements become the markers of worth. We learn to orient our lives around the next goal, the next title, the next accomplishment, believing that fulfillment will finally settle once we reach it. Yet even when the outcome appears, satisfaction often fades quickly. Another goal rises in its place, and the cycle begins again. Over time, this pursuit leaves us weary, because it was never designed to nourish the soul.

Outcomes are only the surface. Beneath every form lies something more fundamental: the energy from which it arose. Creation does not begin with the shape we try to secure, but with the state from which it emerges. It begins with the frequency we embody.

Frequency is the atmosphere of our being—the subtle vibration of our thoughts, emotions, intentions, and the quality of presence with which we inhabit each moment. It is invisible yet formative, subtle yet generative. Just as music can alter the mood of an entire room, the frequency we carry shapes how life meets us. We may desire peace as an outcome, but if we live

103

within the vibration of fear, even peace will feel fragile. We may seek love as an outcome, but if we carry the resonance of unworthiness, love will feel distant or difficult to receive.

This shift changes everything. We are freed from the exhausting burden of controlling how life must unfold. We no longer need to micromanage every detail of becoming. The form may surprise us, but the essence will remain true. To live this way is to remember that life is not a checklist of achievements, but a field of resonance to inhabit.

This is the invitation of conscious creation: to stop defining ourselves by what we achieve, and to begin shaping life through the frequencies we choose to live.

Creation Beyond Control

Much of what we are taught about creation begins with control. We are encouraged to plan, manage, strategize, and force outcomes. We are told that success belongs to those who hold the firmest grip—those who can bend circumstances to their will. On the surface, this approach appears strong, even admirable. We celebrate mastery, mistaking dominance for power and precision for wisdom.

Yet beneath this posture lies an underlying fatigue. Control is heavy. It demands constant vigilance, constant adjustment, constant fear that something might slip away. To live in control is to live braced, as though life itself were an adversary to be subdued. It is no wonder that so many of us, even when surrounded by achievement, feel restless and depleted. We have mistaken tension for stability.

Creation in its truest sense does not arise from control. Control can shape form, but it cannot breathe spirit into it. It can polish surfaces, but it cannot generate depth. Control grasps at outcomes, while creation flows from essence. True creation is resonance—the natural alignment between what we embody and what life reflects.

Resonance cannot be forced, because it is not about bending circumstances to our will. It is about tuning ourselves to the frequency of what we wish to live. Just as one vibration awakens another, so the energy we embody shapes the field around us. Peace calls forth peace. Trust awakens trust. Love multiplies love. Control may mimic the surface, but resonance generates the real.

Consider a river. Control seeks to dam it, to channel it into narrow boundaries, fearing its unpredictability. Resonance is the courage to enter the flow—steering without resisting, trusting that the current knows its way. Control exhausts us because it pits us against life itself. Resonance sustains us because it allows us to move with the greater rhythm already unfolding.

This does not mean we become passive or abandon action. Creation beyond control still involves choice, effort, and responsibility. But the quality of action changes. Choices arise from clarity rather than fear. Effort emerges from coherence rather than desperation. The energy once spent on holding everything together is released into creativity, connection, and meaning.

When we loosen the grip of control, life begins to surprise us. Opportunities appear that could not have been engineered. Connections emerge that no strategy could have produced. The forms may differ from what we imagined, but the essence reflects the resonance we have embodied.

Creation beyond control is not weakness. It is a different kind of power—not the strained power of forcing outcomes, but the steady authority of resonance.

Living by Resonance and Energy

When we release the compulsion to control, we begin to notice what has been shaping our lives all along: resonance. Life does not primarily respond to our plans or demands. It mirrors the energy we carry. What we live inwardly becomes the field we transmit outwardly—and this field shapes how the world responds.

We have all felt this truth without needing language for it. Someone enters a room, and the atmosphere shifts before a word is spoken. Warmth, tension, openness, or contraction becomes palpable. Nothing has happened externally, yet everything has changed. This is resonance—the communication of energy before expression.

Resonance is not limited to people. Spaces hold it. Objects absorb it. Animals sense it instantly. Children respond to it instinctively. Nature reflects it continuously. The world itself is vibrational, and we participate in this living exchange—transmitting what we embody, receiving what surrounds us.

When we live in fear, life often reflects fear back to us. Possibilities feel scarce. Relationships feel strained. Circumstances feel heavy. Not because life has turned against us, but because we are tuned to that frequency, and so that is what we perceive and reinforce. When we shift—even slightly—into trust or gratitude, life shifts with us. Doors soften. Connections open. The outer form may not change overnight, but our way of meeting it transforms everything.

This is why outcomes so often disappoint. Outcomes are surfaces. They are forms we reach for, hoping they will deliver what only frequency can provide. We may attain the promotion, yet still feel insecure. We may enter the relationship, yet remain guarded. No outcome can override the resonance from which it was born.

But when the frequency changes, even the simplest forms feel rich. An ordinary meal becomes abundant in gratitude. A small step feels expansive when taken in joy. A quiet conversation becomes luminous when carried in presence. The form may be modest, but the resonance infuses it with meaning.

To live by resonance is not to ignore the outer world. It is to see it as reflection. What we embody, we amplify. What we carry, we invite. Life responds not as reward or judgment, but as resonance.

Vibration in Thought, Emotion, Intention, and Presence

Frequency is not abstract. It is lived. It is shaped moment by moment by the inner currents we carry—our thoughts, our emotions, our intentions, and the quality of presence through which we move.

Thought carries vibration.
A thought rooted in fear tightens perception
and narrows possibility.
A thought rooted in trust opens space
and widens what seems possible.
Thought is not a fleeting event;
it is a seed that shapes the field in which life unfolds.

Emotion carries vibration.
Emotion is energy in motion,
coloring how we enter each moment.
Fear contracts. Gratitude expands.
Anger, when denied, distorts;
when honored, clarifies.
Joy brightens the field around us.
Emotion does not dictate outcomes,

but it tunes the resonance we emit.
Intention carries vibration.
Intention is the posture of the soul.
It is not demand, nor fantasy, but orientation.
Two people may take identical actions, yet the resonance
differs entirely depending on the intention beneath them.
When intention arises from alignment rather than
fragmentation, it infuses action with coherence.

Presence carries vibration.
Presence is the field that holds everything else.
It is the way we inhabit the moment—
scattered or grounded, guarded or open, hurried or receptive.
Presence gives tone to thought, emotion, and intention.
It is the ground that allows frequency to become embodied
rather than theoretical.

When we begin to see vibration as the lived texture of our inner
life, creation becomes tangible. Frequency is no longer mystical
or distant. It is immediate, intimate, and always shaped from
within.

Here, a deeper truth emerges:
alignment creates coherence within;
coherence expressed becomes congruence;
and when coherence meets life, resonance is born.

This brings us to the next movement of the journey:
Freedom in vibration.

Not freedom from challenge,
but freedom from the belief
that life must be controlled into place.

Freedom born not of force,
but of resonance.

This is where the path turns next.

Freedom in Vibration

We often imagine freedom as control over circumstances—the ability to shape life exactly as we wish, to remove uncertainty, to guarantee stability. But this freedom is conditional. It lasts only as long as conditions cooperate. When circumstances shift, fear returns.

True freedom is not found in controlling the outer world. It is found in choosing the frequency through which we meet it.

When we remember this, the grip of fear loosens. We no longer see ourselves as victims of circumstance or as rulers who must dominate it. Instead, we recognize ourselves as participants in creation, shaping reality through the energy we embody. Outer turbulence still arises, but they no longer define us. The outer form may change, but the inner frequency we live can remain steady.

Freedom in vibration is the ability to live joy amid uncertainty, peace amid change, gratitude amid impermanence. It is the realization that our well-being is not determined by external outcomes, but by the resonance we choose to inhabit.

This freedom reshapes everything. Decisions feel less pressured because we trust the frequency we carry. Relationships shift because we are no longer seeking completion outside ourselves.

Challenges become openings rather than fixed meanings, because we sense the invitation to embody trust, courage, or compassion more deeply.

Freedom in vibration does not erase action; it liberates it.
Action arising from contraction narrows possibility.
Action arising from coherence opens space.
Words spoken from tension close the heart.
Words spoken from presence open connection.

When we live in vibrational freedom, every step becomes a creative act. We no longer measure ourselves by outcomes alone, because we recognize that outcomes are reflections, not origins. Worth is no longer something to earn; it emerges naturally from what we embody.

This is why rest becomes possible—not the rest of withdrawal, but the rest of alignment. It is the rest that comes when we are no longer bracing against life or monitoring every outcome. The nervous system softens. The heart unclenches. The mind releases its vigilance. We are no longer holding ourselves rigid against uncertainty; we are rooted in resonance and moving with what unfolds.

This is freedom not as control, but as coherence.
Not as dominance, but as alignment.
Not as mastery of form, but as embodiment of essence.

Closing Reflection

To shift from outcomes to frequencies is to enter a different way of living—one that no longer binds worth to achievement, but roots meaning in embodiment. Control offers the illusion of power, but it is unsustainable and exhausting. Resonance, by contrast, is grounded and enduring. It carries us without force, because it flows from the truth of who we are.

Creation beyond control invites us to stop confusing effort with power. It reveals that alignment, not tension, shapes life. When we live by resonance, we discover that what we carry inwardly radiates outwardly, shaping the world we move through. Thoughts, emotions, intentions, and presence become the subtle architecture of reality. Life does not primarily answer our demands; it responds to our vibration.

Freedom, then, is not found in outcomes alone. Outcomes rise and fall, appear and fade. Freedom is found in the frequency we choose to inhabit—in joy carried through uncertainty, in peace embodied amid change, in love expressed even when conditions are imperfect. This is freedom in its deepest form: the freedom to create not by controlling life, but by embodying the essence we wish to live.

Yet this freedom is never self-contained. Frequencies ripple outward. What we embody becomes part of the field we share. Our resonance moves through relationships, communities, and the living world itself.

To live aligned is not only personal transformation;
it is participation in a larger dance of creation.

So the path turns once more. Having remembered the power of vibration, we now step into its next unfolding—the dance of co-creation. No longer as solitary creators, but as beings woven into a living web of resonance, where Spirit, self, and world meet in shared becoming.

Alignment has brought us into coherence.
Resonance now invites us into communion.

And the journey continues.

Chapter 11

The Dance of Co-Creation

The dance is not about leading or following,
but learning how to move as one.
— Kea Rivers

Creation has never been solitary. Even in our most private moments of reflection, decision, or longing, we are not creating alone. We are participating in a living field that stretches beyond what we can see. Every thought carries a tone. Every emotion shapes an atmosphere. Every act, however small, sends ripples through a wider fabric of becoming. Whether we are conscious of it or not, our very being contributes to the ongoing movement of creation.

This realization is both humbling and liberating. It reminds us that our lives matter not only for what we accomplish, but for what we embody. It also reminds us that we are never isolated authors of our lives. We are always in relationship—with Spirit, with the rhythms of life, and with one another. Every moment is an exchange, a conversation, a resonance unfolding between inner and outer worlds.

This is why the image of dance feels so true.

A dance is not rigid or predetermined. It is responsive, fluid, alive. It requires listening as much as movement, yielding as much as leading. Sometimes we are carried; sometimes we initiate. Sometimes we stumble, and the rhythm pauses — only to re-emerge in a new form. To live as co-creators is to step into this dance, not choreographed by control, but guided by resonance.

The beauty of the dance lies not in uniformity, but in interplay. Each of us brings a distinct frequency, perspective, and way of moving. Alone, each expression is partial. Together, they weave something larger, richer, more whole. Just as a dance gains depth through exchange between partners, creation gains meaning through the harmony of distinct expressions.

To awaken to co-creation is to move beyond isolation.

Life is not something happening to us, nor something we must single-handedly manage and master. Life is alive, responsive, attuned. Spirit is not distant but intimate, pulsing through ordinary moments. Others are not merely obstacles or competitors, but mirrors and companions in the unfolding of meaning. Even disruption and loss — though difficult — can become part of the choreography, shaping us in ways that deepen the music of our becoming.

This is the invitation of co-creation: to enter the dance fully, not as solitary performers, but as participants in a larger movement. To trust the rhythm even when it is unfamiliar. To recognize that the dance is greater than any one of us alone.

To live this way is to live awake—awake to our own resonance, awake to the field we are weaving with, awake to the truth that creation is always shared.

So we begin with the partners who are always present in this dance.

Weaving with Spirit, Life, and Others

To co-create is to recognize that we are never weaving the fabric of life alone. Every thought, every choice, every vibration that flows through us is already in dialogue with something larger —Spirit, life, and others. These companions are always present, whether or not we notice them. To live as conscious creators is to enter relationship with them deliberately, reverently, and attentively.

With Spirit

Spirit is the quiet pulse beneath breath, the stillness beneath thought, the spark that rises before language forms. Spirit does not direct; it invites. It calls us toward coherence, whispering through intuition, synchronicity, and moments of unexpected clarity. Spirit is not only beyond us; it is within us—meeting us not as distant authority, but as intimate collaborator.

When we attune to Spirit, creation shifts from effort to communion. What once felt like something we had to push begins to unfold through listening. We discover that the dance of creation begins not in control, but in relationship.

With Life

Life is an ever-present partner in the dance. Often we treat it as something to manage or brace against, fearing its unpredictability. Yet life carries its own intelligence, its own rhythms of emergence and retreat, expansion and contraction. When we push against these rhythms, we exhaust ourselves.

When we learn to listen, we begin to see meaning in the seasons —in pauses and accelerations, in detours and openings. Life is not diverting us; it is conversing with us. To co-create with life is to recognize that even before we were aware of the dance, life was already inviting us into a story alive with possibility.

With Others

Others enter our lives as mirrors, companions, catalysts, and teachers. Some remain for a lifetime; others appear only briefly. Yet every encounter carries invitation. A word of kindness can shift a day. A conflict can reveal a hidden truth. A shared vision can give rise to something neither could create alone.

Others reflect both our light and our shadows. They reveal what is emerging within us and what remains unintegrated. To co-create with others is not to merge or compete, but to bring our authentic frequency into relationship, trusting that together we weave patterns of meaning that extend beyond what we can see.

When Spirit, life, and others are seen together, co-creation becomes clear: Spirit offers pulse, life provides rhythm, others bring form and movement. We are both thread and weaver, participant and collaborator.

Yet to truly enter this dance, something deeper is required.

We must learn the art of surrender.

The Art of Surrender and Partnership

If co-creation is the dance of relationship, surrender is the posture that allows the dance to flow.

Without surrender, we stiffen. We insist on directing every step, shaping life into narrow forms, demanding that Spirit confirm our plans and others mirror our expectations. In that rigidity, movement becomes constrained. We may achieve control, but we lose communion.

True surrender is not collapse. It is trust.

It is the willingness to loosen our grip on certainty and allow ourselves to be guided by rhythms we cannot fully predict. It is choosing partnership over dominance, listening as deeply as we act, allowing the steady pull of Spirit to shape our becoming as naturally as our desires shape our choices.

This surrender is active, not passive. It requires courage, because it invites vulnerability. It asks us to release outcomes we once clung to, to welcome pathways we did not plan, to remain open when clarity is incomplete. Yet in that openness, we rediscover our connection to the larger field of creation, where we are never moving alone.

Partnership emerges from this trust.

To co-create is to allow Spirit to inspire, life to guide, and others to contribute. Sometimes we lead; sometimes we follow. Sometimes the rhythm accelerates; sometimes it slows. The art is not mastery, but responsiveness—remaining attuned to what the moment calls for.

Surrender also expands perception. It humbles us, reminding us that no single perspective holds the whole. We may grasp only one thread while Spirit, life, and others weave patterns beyond our view. When we surrender, we make room for those unseen threads. The tapestry reveals itself as more intricate, more luminous, more alive than anything we could orchestrate alone.

So surrender becomes not loss, but release.

It frees us from the exhaustion of control, from the pressure to know every answer, from the illusion of solitary authorship. In surrender, partnership deepens, and creation becomes not a strain we shoulder alone, but a current we join.

And when partnership deepens, something unexpected emerges: joy.

The Joy of the Shared Unfolding

When we loosen our grip on control and enter partnership with Spirit, life, and others, we begin to experience a steadier, more grounded joy—not the thrill of achievement, but the delight of shared unfolding.

This joy begins with the recognition that we are supported.

When insight arises naturally, when clarity arrives without strain, when intuition guides us beyond what logic could predict, we sense Spirit moving through us. What once felt like pressure to produce becomes an invitation to respond. In that responsiveness, joy emerges naturally.

Life joins in this joy as well.

What once seemed random begins to reveal rhythm. Doors close and open. Delays deepen roots. Encounters redirect paths. We begin to see that even the unexpected has shaped us with intelligence and care. Joy arises not because life always gives us what we hoped for, but because we begin to trust that life is working with us, not against us.

Others bring this joy into visible form.

In moments of connection, collaboration, conflict, and reconciliation, we discover that creation is richer when shared. A conversation sparks insight neither could reach alone. A challenge reveals hidden strength. A presence steadies us when our own ground feels uncertain. Others expand the field of what is possible simply by being who they are.

The joy of shared unfolding is not reserved for grand moments. It lives in ordinary exchanges—laughter, silence, presence, attention. It arises when we allow ourselves to participate fully, without needing to control the outcome.

Even mystery becomes part of the joy.

We do not always understand how threads connect or why rhythms unfold as they do. Yet within the not-knowing, there is a subtle delight—the sense that something meaningful is being woven beyond our sight. The unknown becomes not a threat, but an invitation to listen more deeply.

This joy does not deny difficulty. It does not erase sorrow or seasons of letting go. But even in those spaces, the shared unfolding continues. Spirit offers steady presence. Life maintains its rhythm. Others bring companionship. Joy, here, is not the absence of challenge, but the presence of connection.

This is the joy of co-creation: the realization that life is not a solo performance, but a shared dance. We are not merely shaping life; we are being shaped by it. And in that mutual shaping, meaning arises.

Closing Reflection

Co-creation is the remembrance that we are never weaving

alone.

Spirit moves as the unseen thread. Life provides the living loom. Others become the fibers that cross our own. Together, these strands form a tapestry far greater than any single hand could design. What once appeared random reveals rhythm. What once felt like interruption becomes invitation. The pattern deepens, and we discover our place within it.

Surrender teaches us how to enter this weave—not as controllers of the thread, but as participants in its flow. In loosening our grip on outcomes, we discover a deeper strength: the strength of yielding to the current that has always been carrying us.

Partnership steadies us within the dance. Spirit whispers, life responds, others mirror—and we are shaped by their presence as much as we shape in return. Even in moments of tension or uncertainty, we remain held within a larger choreography of becoming.

Joy becomes the hidden music of the dance.

Without joy, creation hardens into performance. With joy, it becomes alive. Joy does not deny shadow; it moves with it, reminding us that even within uncertainty there is wonder, even within complexity there is meaning.

This is the essence of co-creation: to be woven, guided, and lifted by a movement larger than ourselves. To yield without disappearing. To partner without losing our voice. To dance without needing to control the music.

Yet to glimpse this truth is only the beginning.

The deeper call is embodiment.

To let our choices become offerings.
To let our presence become communion.
To live as if every breath were sacred,
every step already belonging to the rhythm of Spirit,
every act of creation shimmering with the presence of the Divine.

And so the path turns once more.

From the dance of co-creation, we move into the mystery of Embodied Divinity—not as an idea to understand, but as a life to inhabit.

Chapter 12

Embodied Divinity

The altar is not a place one goes. It is a way one lives.
— *Kea Rivers*

To speak of divinity is to speak of what is most real, most alive, most essential in us. It is not a lofty abstraction locked away in theology, nor a prize reserved for saints or sages. Divinity is not distant—it is intimate. It is the breath moving in and out of our lungs, the sustaining strength that carries us when we falter, the presence that holds us in moments too deep for words.

And yet, for much of our lives, we forget. We learn to divide the world into "sacred" and "ordinary," to place holiness in temples, rituals, and prayers while labeling the rest of life as mundane. But this division is a mirage. The deeper truth is this: nothing is ordinary. Every space we enter, every action we take, every relationship we tend holds the potential to reveal the sacred—if we have eyes to see.

Embodied Divinity is not about reaching beyond our humanity. It is about remembering that the sacred and the human have never been separate. Divinity shines not in spite of our humanity, but through it. It is present in the tenderness of sorrow and the brightness of laughter, in the courage to remain steady in difficulty and the humility to ask for help. It is present in the simple act of showing up—living with awareness, choosing love where fear might otherwise take root.

This embodiment is not achieved through effort, but through remembrance. It is not about earning a place in the sacred, but recognizing we have never left it. The sacred saturates the whole of life: the meal prepared with care, the child's hand held in reassurance, the quiet prayer whispered in a crowded room. When we awaken to this, life itself becomes a temple, and daily living becomes the offering.

To embody divinity is to allow Spirit's presence to flow not only through moments of inspiration, but through the smallest rhythms of existence. It is to let our choices, words, and actions carry the resonance of what is most true. It is to become—not in perfection, but in authenticity—a living expression of the Divine essence that has always been within us.

This is the culmination of the journey: not only seeking, not only finding, not only co-creating, but being. Being awake. Being aligned. Being transparent to the sacred that shines through us. Here, creation is no longer simply what we do, but who we are. Every breath becomes sacred ground. Every interaction becomes an opening to honor the Divine within ourselves and within others.

This is Embodied Divinity: not the destination of the journey, but the deepening of it—the point where we stop searching for the sacred outside ourselves and begin living as its expression.

It begins here—not in grand gestures or extraordinary moments, but in the fabric of daily life. For if the Divine truly lives within us, then every moment carries the possibility of revelation. The ordinary becomes sacred when seen with awakened eyes.

The Sacred in the Ordinary

If the Divine truly lives within us, then it must be discoverable not only in rare moments of transcendence, but also in the pulse of daily life. The sacred is not confined to special days, mountaintops, or fleeting visions. It is infused into the ordinary: in the breaths we take, the choices we make, the kindness we extend, the tasks we complete without fanfare.

We often miss it because we've been taught to expect the sacred to arrive with grandeur—in unmistakable signs or dramatic awakenings. Yet more often, Spirit comes unassumingly, clothed in simplicity: light falling across a familiar room, laughter interrupting an ordinary day, silence settling when the world pauses for a breath. These moments rarely announce themselves. They require us to notice.

Think of how washing dishes can become an act of reverence when done with attention—warm water on your hands reminding you of the nourishment just received. Think of how sitting with a loved one in silence can feel like communion, even without words, because presence itself becomes the offering. Think of how walking outdoors, when fully noticed, can unveil a thousand small wonders: the curve of clouds, the song of birds, the way your breath falls in step with your stride.

The sacred is hidden in plain sight, waiting for awareness to awaken. When our seeing shifts, the mundane reveals itself as holy ground. The table becomes communion. The bed becomes sanctuary. The conversation becomes sacrament. The body itself becomes a living temple, carrying the spark of Divinity through every gesture and breath.

This recognition changes us. We no longer divide life into "spiritual" and "ordinary," as though the sacred could be limited to certain times and places. We begin to live as though all of life is infused with presence. Paying bills, raising children, preparing food, grieving loss, celebrating milestones—all of it belongs. All of it is touched by the same sacred breath.

The sacred in the ordinary does not deny life's hardships. It does not pretend struggle is unreal. But it reframes our relationship to what is difficult. Even in hard seasons, the presence of the Divine can be felt—in the resilience to take another step, in the love that finds us when we did not expect it, in the strength that rises when we thought we were empty. To live with this awareness is to discover that nothing is beyond the reach of Divinity.

Perhaps this is the truest invitation of Embodied Divinity: to stop seeking the Sacred as something separate, and begin to see it shimmering in the midst of everything we already are and everything we already do.

As this awareness deepens, a question emerges from within: if the Sacred is not separate from the ordinary, then who are we but its living vessels? The invitation is not only to recognize the Sacred in life, but to recognize ourselves as its expression—to live as the "I Am," the Divine made visible through our very being.

Living as the "I Am"

To live as the "I Am" is to root ourselves in the ground of being —in the essence that remains when every role, label, and circumstance falls away. Beneath the shifting surface of identity —parent, partner, worker, friend, leader, dreamer—there is something more constant, more spacious, more enduring. It is the presence that simply is. The "I Am" is not something we create or achieve; it is the truth that has always been.

These two small words carry immeasurable power. Mystics across traditions have pointed to this: when you say and feel "I Am," you open the door to the natural flow of Divine life within you. It is not a statement of ego, but of essence—the release of what has always been present. "I Am" is not merely language; it is living current. When we inhabit this awareness, we are not calling the Divine from afar; we are allowing the Divine to live, breathe, and create through us here and now.

This truth is deceptively simple. To say "I Am" is to stand in existence without adornment, without justification. It is to remember that who we are at the core needs no proof. We are not "I am what I do," nor "I am what I have," nor "I am what others say about me." Those are passing garments—sometimes beautiful, sometimes heavy—but never the essence. The essence is simply: I Am.

When we begin to live from this place, something loosens. The anxiety of performance relaxes, because our worth is no longer tethered to achievement. The fear of rejection softens, because our identity no longer depends on approval. Even disappointment takes on a different meaning, because it no longer threatens who we are—it becomes part of life's shaping, part of our ongoing learning.

This awareness also transforms how we see others. When we look past roles, masks, and protective patterns, we begin to glimpse the same presence shining through them. Their essence, too, whispers "I Am." Even those who challenge us carry the same spark, however hidden. Living as the "I Am" draws us into reverence, reminding us that every interaction is sacred ground: divinity meeting Divinity, presence meeting Presence.

And this truth is not meant to remain abstract. The "I Am" must be embodied. It is not merely a phrase to repeat, but a way of inhabiting life. It takes shape in the way we speak with integrity, act with compassion, and align our outer living with our inner truth. To live as the "I Am" is to let every breath, every word, every gesture be infused with the awareness that we are expressions of the Divine.

There will still be seasons of intensity. Sorrow will still visit, fear will still rise, uncertainty will still test us. Yet when we are anchored in the "I Am," we discover a steadiness that outlasts every season. We may bend, but we are not undone. We may grieve, but our center holds. For beneath it all, the ground remains: I Am.

This is the deepest remembering: not that we will one day become divine, but that we already are. Not that the Sacred lives somewhere else, but that it breathes within us. To live as the "I Am" is to awaken to who we have always been—and to let that truth shine through the whole of our lives.

Once we begin to live as the "I Am," the ordinary world changes. Daily life is no longer separate from the Sacred—it becomes its expression. The meals we prepare, the work we offer, the love we give and receive—all of it becomes altar. All of it becomes a living offering.

Everyday Life as Altar

When the truth of the "I Am" begins to saturate awareness, something subtle yet profound unfolds: the veil between sacred and ordinary dissolves. We no longer look for the Divine in far-off places while dismissing daily life as trivial. Instead, we discover that everything belongs. Every act, every moment, every encounter has the potential to shine with the presence of Spirit. Life itself becomes the altar upon which the Sacred reveals itself.

To live this way is to stop waiting for sacredness and begin recognizing it everywhere. The Sacred is not confined to hushed sanctuaries or rare mystical moments. It is present in the warmth of morning light falling across a cluttered table. It is present in tired but loving hands preparing dinner after a long day. It is present in the steadfast courage it takes to meet sorrow honestly, without running.

This kind of seeing transforms routines into rituals of devotion. Folding laundry becomes a practice of care, each garment a reminder of the bodies it clothes and the lives it touches. Writing an email with integrity becomes an offering of clarity and respect. Even pausing for a single mindful breath becomes an act of reverence—a way of remembering: I Am here. Life is here. The Sacred is here.

The altar of everyday life is not about perfection, but intention. It is not about performing sacredness, but living awake to it. The simplest acts, when infused with presence, ripple with lasting significance: a kind word spoken when none was expected, a silent blessing offered for someone who will never know, a laugh shared in the middle of an ordinary day.

These moments are not small; they are the heart of what it means to live as a vessel of Divinity.

The altar does not exclude difficulty. It widens to hold it. When grief is laid bare, when anger is acknowledged without harm, when longing is named honestly, these too become offerings. The altar is large enough to hold the whole of who we are—not only the parts we feel proud to show. To bring our tender humanity to the altar is to discover that Spirit meets us there— not with rejection, but with embrace.

Over time, this way of living shapes us. We stop rushing past the ordinary, reaching only for what seems extraordinary. We stop dividing life into compartments—sacred on Sunday, forgetful on Monday; prayer in solitude, absence in daily living. Instead, we begin to live seamlessly: every space becomes sanctuary, every task becomes an offering, every breath becomes part of the great liturgy of existence.

The altar is not somewhere we visit. It is not a place we go. It is who we are when we live with awareness. To live as the "I Am" is to recognize that our very being—in its joys, its challenges, its ordinariness—is already sacred. Life itself is the offering. Presence is the expression.

Closing Reflection

We began this movement by exploring alignment—learning that creation flows most powerfully when thought, word, and deed move in harmony. We released the illusion of control and discovered the deeper current of resonance, living by frequency rather than forcing outcomes. We stepped into the dance of co-creation, realizing that life is not ours to manage alone, but ours to meet in rhythm, surrender, and trust. And now we arrive at the heart of it all: Embodied Divinity.

To see the Sacred in the ordinary is to open our eyes to a truth that was never absent—only overlooked. The Divine is not waiting in some distant realm; it is here, pulsing through the most everyday of moments. It is here in the softness of a morning breath, in the exchange of a kind word, in the resilience of continuing through difficulty. Nothing is outside its reach. Nothing is too small to carry its light.

To live as the "I Am" is to root ourselves in the unshakable ground of being. It is to remember that we are not defined by what we do, by what we own, or by how others see us. Our essence is deeper than circumstance, deeper than identity, deeper even than time. It is presence itself—the spark of Divinity that whispers: I Am. When we live from this place, our lives cease to be performances seeking validation. They become transparent expressions of truth.

When this awareness enters daily life, everything becomes offering. Every act, no matter how small, can be a gesture of devotion. Every word spoken in love, every task done with presence, every breath received with gratitude becomes part of the altar.

This is the essence of Embodied Divinity: not that we escape our humanity, but that we inhabit it more fully and let it reveal its sacred depths. We discover that joy is sacred—and so is sorrow. Ease is sacred—and so is growth that comes through difficulty. Ordinary life is not an obstacle to the Divine; it is the place where Divinity most longs to be expressed.

And this is not an ending. It is a living rhythm—a continual movement of remembering and forgetting, opening and returning, grounding and rising again. What we have touched here is not a conclusion, but the beginning of a deeper spiral.

Part IV invites us into that next movement: integration — wholeness in motion. Not a static state, not a fixed endpoint, but a life that keeps unfolding into greater depth. Seeking, finding, and being are not stages we outgrow; they are rhythms we learn to weave into the ongoing choreography of life.

So we step across this threshold carrying one simple, world-changing knowing: life itself is sacred ground—and we are not separate from its sacredness. The altar is already beneath our feet. The spiral already moves within us. Now the invitation is to live that rhythm—to let the human and the Divine meet in us, until they are no longer two.

And what was remembered became the way of living.

And so the journey flows on…
returning you to wholeness again and again.

Part IV - Integration: Wholeness in Motion

The eternal rhythm—
cycles of forgetting and remembering,
being and becoming.

Chapter 13

Life as Sacred Spiral

The spiral transforms the form,
but never diminishes the essence of who we are.
— *Kea Rivers*

Wholeness is not a fixed state of arrival, nor a permanent crown to be worn. It is alive — breathing, moving, unfolding through us in rhythms both tender and fierce. It cannot be measured by checklists or milestones. It cannot be pinned down as a final accomplishment. Wholeness is motion: an ever-turning spiral that carries us deeper into the truth of who we are.

We are often taught to imagine growth as linear — a path of ascent, each step an improvement, each milestone proof of progress. But life reveals a more mysterious rhythm. Again and again, we circle back to familiar terrain: old questions, old patterns, old longing. At first, it can feel discouraging, as though we have returned to where we began. But the spiral shows us something different: though the landscape looks familiar, we have changed. We meet what once unsettled us with new steadiness. We hear what once confused us with new clarity. The spiral deepens us, reminding us that revisiting is not regression — it is ripening.

The sacred spiral is not a metaphor to admire. It is a way of

139

inhabiting life—where forgetting and remembering are woven into how we grow. This rhythm honors our humanity. Forgetting is not a defect in the design; it is part of the design. In the spiral, forgetting is not avoided but held, because return is always possible. Doubt, struggle, and repetition are not detours; they are invitations. The spiral says: you will drift, and you will return. Each return draws you closer to integration, not because truth was ever lost, but because you are now able to carry it more fully. In this way, remembering ripens into wholeness.

Wholeness, then, is not perfection. It is not an end-state free of shadow or challenge. Wholeness is spaciousness—the capacity to hold light and dark, joy and sorrow, certainty and unknowing within the same embrace. The spiral teaches us to include, not exclude; to weave, not divide. It shows us that nothing is wasted, that every turn belongs to the rhythm of becoming.

To live as sacred spiral is to trust the ongoing motion of life. It is to welcome each season—the rising and the falling, the remembering and the forgetting—as part of a sacred pattern. It is to stop demanding that life be a straight line of "progress," and instead bow to the wisdom of cycles.

When we live this way, integration ceases to be about arrival and becomes about weaving. We gather the threads of our experiences—the seeking, the finding, the being—and allow them to spiral together into a life of depth and resonance. Even when we feel we are circling the same ground, the spiral reveals that we are never in the same place twice. We are always being carried deeper, always being drawn closer to the essence of who we are.

The spiral is not our enemy. It is our teacher. It reveals that wholeness is not an achievement, but a rhythm—not a possession, but a continual becoming. And when we begin to live this truth, the pressure to reach an endpoint dissolves. What remains is the invitation to walk the spiral with presence, courage, and trust—knowing that it is leading us, always, toward home.

Within this spiral, one rhythm rises again and again: forgetting and remembering. This forgetting is not amnesia. It is a drifting from presence—a turning away from inner knowing rather than a loss of truth. We forget who we are, only to be reminded. We drift from the center, only to be called back. Far from being a flaw, this cycle is part of the soul's unfolding—the very way the spiral carries us deeper into what has always been true.

Cycles of Forgetting and Remembering

From the moment we enter this world, a veil of forgetfulness rests upon us. This is not a sign of inadequacy; it is the human condition—the very field in which remembering becomes possible. Forgetting and remembering are not accidents. They are rhythms of the spiral. And they do not happen once and then resolve. They repeat throughout our lives, each return deepening our capacity to live from being.

Life itself participates in this rhythm. Beauty, loss, conflict, love —all of it becomes mirror. Some experiences draw us into forgetting, pulling us into distraction or survival. Others awaken remembering, opening us into stillness, clarity, or reverence. And often, the same experience can do both: a hardship that initially disorients us may later become the doorway through which remembering enters.

Remembering may feel like grace—and it is—but it also asks something of us: a willingness to pause, to turn inward, to attend to the deeper truth beneath the noise. Not effort in the sense of strain, but effort in the sense of intention—the steady turning of the soul back toward its own center.

To live as human is to live within cycles. Day gives way to night. Seasons rise and fall. Breath expands and releases. The soul, too, follows its rhythm: the ebb of forgetting and the flow of remembering. We may resist this motion, longing for permanent clarity, wishing we could hold every insight without slipping. Yet the spiral whispers: forgetting and remembering are not detours. They are the way.

Forgetting often begins subtly—as distraction, a slow drift into constant motion. We tell ourselves we'll return to what matters later, and before we know it, days have passed and presence feels far away. Other times, forgetting arrives like a wave— grief, fear, or hardship sweeping through and pulling us under.

In both cases, we may feel separated from the living center of truth, convinced it has disappeared.

But forgetting never erases what is real. The truth of who we are remains — steady as the moon behind shifting clouds. Even when obscured, it waits: patient, unshaken, undiminished. Forgetting may veil, but it cannot destroy.

Remembering, then, is homecoming. Sometimes it arrives in an instant — awe before beauty, the tenderness of a loved one's embrace, a silence that opens unexpectedly within us. Other times it comes slowly, shaped through small acts of return: a breath, a pause, a simple kindness that reawakens what is true. However it comes, remembering is never harsh. It does not scold us for drifting. It simply whispers: *You are still here. You have always been here.*

The spiral ensures that each cycle carries us deeper. What once looked like going backward reveals itself as deepening, because when we return, we return changed. We come back with more humility, more compassion, more capacity to see with gentle eyes. Forgetting can soften arrogance by loosening our certainty and reopen tenderness. Remembering restores us — not because truth was ever lost, but because we are now ready to live it with greater depth.

Over time, we learn to meet forgetting with reverence. We stop treating it as an enemy and begin to see it as part of the rhythm that strengthens us. Forgetting teaches tenderness — toward ourselves and toward others. It reminds us that presence is not proven by never drifting, but by returning, again and again.

To live in this cycle is to release the illusion of permanence and receive the beauty of motion. It is to trust that even when we lose our bearings, the path is still holding us. Forgetting is never the end. It is often the doorway through which remembering enters.

Forgetting and remembering are the heartbeat of the spiral. They do not weaken the soul's journey—they deepen it. Wholeness is not linear or static; it is alive and rhythmic. Each return draws us closer to the essence of who we have always been, not by avoiding the spiral, but by inhabiting it fully.

Here the spiral reveals its deeper wisdom: it does not waste what we once judged as "mistake," shadow, or detour. By returning us to the places we left behind, it invites us to gather what was scattered and welcome it home. Light and dark, joy and sorrow, clarity and doubt—no longer enemies to separate, but companions held within a larger becoming.

This is the gift of non-linearity: it teaches us that depth matters more than progress.

The Beauty of Non-Linearity

Straight lines promise certainty. They reassure us that if we simply keep moving forward, life will deliver us to some imagined arrival: success, peace, enlightenment, completion.

But straight lines are illusions. They belong to blueprints and maps—not to the living soul.

Look to nature. Rivers meander. Trees grow in rings. Seasons return. Even galaxies spiral, vast and unhurried, reminding us that the architecture of existence resists linearity. Why would our lives be any different?

Yet we are conditioned to distrust this rhythm. We are taught that returning to an old pattern is "backsliding," that pausing is weakness, that circling back proves we haven't learned. We measure our worth by how far we appear to have traveled. But what if wholeness cannot be measured in progress? What if it can only be known by depth?

Non-linearity asks us to shift our gaze. Instead of seeing return as setback, we begin to recognize it as deepening. What we encounter may look familiar, but we are not the same. The terrain has not changed, yet the one walking through it has. This is the quiet beauty of the spiral: we meet old places with new eyes—and discover layers we could not see before.

There is mercy in this rhythm. It frees us from the tyranny of perfectionism, from the inner voice that says, *You should be farther along by now.* The spiral answers gently: *You are exactly where you need to be. Each turn belongs. Each return is sacred.*

To embrace non-linearity is to bow to the wisdom of life itself. The pause holds purpose. The detour carries intelligence. The resurfacing of an old tenderness is not a verdict against you—it may be a sign that you are finally safe enough to meet it with compassion. Even seasons of stillness are weaving something essential beneath the surface.

When we begin to trust this pattern, life softens. We stop forcing ourselves to move faster than the soul's rhythm. We stop comparing our path to others', measuring our worth against their timelines. We begin to see the sacred artistry of our own spiral unfolding in its perfect timing. And in that recognition, a new kind of peace rises—not the peace of arrival, but the peace of being carried.

Because in the spiral, growth is not a march. It is a dance. Healing is not a linear ascent. It is a weaving. Awakening is not one moment held forever. It is a rhythm of drifting and returning. Wholeness is not a static state—it is an ongoing spiral: alive, dynamic, endlessly deepening.

So the spiral invites us to more than acceptance. It invites us to embrace it—to walk its curves with trust rather than resistance, to honor its rhythm rather than fight against it. To see the spiral not as an obstacle, but as the sacred path itself.

This is where the journey turns next: learning to live with open hands along the spiral way.

Embracing the Spiral Path

To truly embrace the spiral path is to change how we see

everything: progress, timing, setbacks, even ourselves. We are no longer bound to the belief that worth is measured by constant ascent. We are freed from the illusion that life should be a neat sequence of improvements. Instead, we begin to recognize the grace of circling, the wisdom of pausing, the sacredness of return.

The spiral path teaches us that depth matters more than distance. A straight line might take us farther on a map, but the spiral carries us deeper into the ground of our being. Each turn presses wisdom into the soul, like rings forming in a tree trunk —invisible from the outside, yet unmistakable in their strength. From the surface, our lives may look like repetition. But inwardly, we know the truth: each return has expanded us, carving new spaciousness, new tenderness, new clarity.

The spiral teaches us that depth matters more than progress. A straight line may take us farther on a map, but the spiral carries us deeper into the ground of our being. Each turn presses wisdom into the soul like rings forming in a tree—invisible from the outside, unmistakable in their strength. From the surface, our lives may look repetitive. But inwardly, we know the truth: each return has expanded us, carving new spaciousness, new tenderness, new clarity.

There is a radical kindness in embracing the spiral. It invites gentleness when we falter, when we drift, when we find ourselves returning to familiar ground. Instead of shame, we offer compassion. Instead of judgment, we extend grace. The spiral reminds us that drifting is not a defect—it is part of the sacred rhythm, the very way remembering takes root.

This path also reshapes how we meet the darker turns of life. Disappointment, loss, confusion do not remove us from the path; they are woven into it. The spiral does not exclude difficulty—it gathers it. When we embrace the spiral, we stop resisting the dark as an enemy and begin to recognize it as a womb: a place where new growth stirs beneath the surface.

To live this way requires trust—trust in the spiral, trust in life, trust in the wisdom moving through us even when the pattern is unclear. Trust is courageous. It asks us to loosen our grip on certainty and linear timelines—to say yes to mystery, yes to process, yes to a rhythm larger than our will.

And when we do, something eases within us. The fear of being out of rhythm loosens. The urgency of proving ourselves softens. We no longer measure ourselves by the straight line of comparison, but by the sacred geometry of our own becoming. We discover a freedom that comes from knowing nothing is wasted—not the pauses, not the setbacks, not even the seasons of forgetting. All of it belongs. All of it is being woven into wholeness.

The spiral path is not always comfortable, but it is always alive with meaning. It is the soul's way of leading us deeper into integration. To embrace it is to live with open hands, open eyes, and an open heart—willing to be shaped, willing to be softened, willing to be transformed.

It is to say: *I do not need life to be a straight line. I will walk the spiral —trusting that it is leading me home.*

Closing Reflection

The spiral reveals that life's wisdom is rarely linear. It carries us in rhythms that circle and deepen—rhythms that may resemble repetition on the surface, yet are subtly weaving wholeness beneath. Drifting and returning, forgetting and remembering, are not breaks in the flow. They are sacred pulses of this motion. Each forgetting humbles us into our humanity. Each remembering restores us to what is most true. Together, they keep us supple, open, and alive.

What we once dismissed as delay or detour often holds a hidden invitation. The pauses allow integration. The circling back opens layers we weren't ready to meet before. The non-linear path slows us enough to feel what is real, to see what we once overlooked, to welcome what we once resisted. What looks inefficient through the lens of linear success is, in the language of the soul, perfectly timed.

To embrace the spiral is to loosen the grip of shame—shame about not being "farther along," shame about returning to familiar ground, shame about being human. The spiral teaches us that our humanity is not something to overcome, but the ground of wholeness itself. In our stumbling, our circling, our repeated returns, something deep is being formed: tenderness, depth, and wisdom that can only be lived into, not rushed.

Here the spiral offers its subtle gift: it releases our fixation on progress and returns us to presence. It shifts the question from *How far have I gone?* to *How deeply am I here?* It reminds us that nothing is wasted—not the pauses, not the recalibrations, not even the seasons of forgetting. All of it belongs. All of it is being woven.

And in this recognition, a gentler freedom begins to rise: the freedom to trust our own rhythm, to respect our unfolding, and to rest more fully in the truth that wholeness has been moving within us all along.

Chapter 14

Freedom Through Self-Honoring

Freedom is not found in becoming someone new,
but in no longer abandoning who you already are.
— Kea Rivers

There is a freedom the world rarely teaches us to seek —
a freedom not built on external success or escape, but on
the inward act of honoring ourselves. This freedom does
not depend on circumstances aligning, on perfection being
achieved, or on others finally seeing us clearly. It rises from
within, from the soul's steady knowing that our lives are
worthy of reverence as they are.

Self-honoring is the art of listening inwardly and responding
with gentleness and truth. It is not indulgence, nor is it
selfishness. It is the practice of acknowledging our inherent
worth, of tending to the needs and limits of the body, mind, and
spirit, and of recognizing that the life moving through us is
sacred. To honor the self is to recognize that we, too, are altars
of the sacred.

Self-honoring is the art of listening inwardly and responding
with gentleness and truth. It is not indulgence, nor is it
selfishness. It is the practice of acknowledging inherent worth,
of tending to the needs and limits of body, mind, and spirit, and
of recognizing that the life moving through us is sacred. To

honor the self is to recognize that we, too, are altars of the sacred.

Without self-honoring, life subtly distorts. We perform to meet expectations even when those performances gradually drain our vitality. We silence our truth to preserve belonging, only to feel unseen in the very places where we long to be known. We push beyond our natural limits because rest has been misnamed as weakness. Over time, the cost becomes clear: outward success paired with inner fragmentation, movement without nourishment, achievement without resonance.

Self-honoring calls us back into coherence. It is a reclamation of authority — the authority to say yes and no from a place of truth, to protect our energy as a sacred resource, and to live by values that resonate with our deepest being. When we begin to honor ourselves in this way, we touch a freedom more enduring than external liberty: the freedom to live undivided, the freedom to belong to ourselves.

This freedom is steady rather than showy. It reveals itself in the courage to rest without apology, to step away from what diminishes us, to welcome joy without self-editing. It is the quiet confidence of showing up as we are, rather than endlessly reshaping ourselves for approval. Worthiness is no longer something to prove; it is recognized as the ground of who we are.

This is where integration takes root. Self-honoring is not an optional practice, but the soil in which wholeness grows. Without it, we continue to offer fragments of ourselves while concealing the rest. With it, every part of us is welcomed into the light, and life begins to move in alignment with our truest essence.

Freedom through self-honoring does not ask us to become someone new. It invites us to stop leaving ourselves behind. It whispers: *Live as you are, for who you are is already enough.* And in that remembering, a spaciousness opens—a freedom as wide and quiet as the sky.

This is where the path shifts from insight into lived expression. For self-honoring is not only inward; it must take form. It asks for the courage to bring who we are into the world without disguise—to speak with our own voice, to stand in our own skin. Its first outward breath is authenticity.

The Courage of Authenticity

Authenticity is the soul's call to live undivided. It asks us to gather the scattered aspects of who we are—the public self and the private self, the confident self and the uncertain self—and allow them to move together. To live authentically is to let inner truth shape outer expression, so that life no longer contradicts itself.

This is rarely easy. From early on, we learn to wear masks. Some are protective—the smile that conceals overwhelm, the silence that avoids conflict, the performance that ensures acceptance. Others arise from expectation — the good child, the capable one, the selfless giver. Over time, these roles harden into identity, and we forget that they were strategies, not essence. Yet beneath them, the soul remains attentive. It knows when we are living divided. It longs for the simplicity of truth.

The courage of authenticity is the courage to begin laying these masks down — not abruptly or recklessly, but with care. It is the gradual releasing of what constricts, the gentle permission for the unedited self to breathe. Authenticity is not exposure for its own sake; it is alignment. It is the process of remembering who we are beneath adaptation and allowing that self to be seen.

This courage is steady. It often begins in small choices: telling the truth when it would be easier to deflect, honoring limits instead of overriding them, allowing joy or grief to be visible without explanation. Each act may seem modest, but together they weave a life of coherence.

Authenticity also asks tenderness. It is not truth unheld or unexamined, but truth carried with care. True authenticity softens rather than hardens. It removes the weight of pretense and reveals a strength that does not rely on armor. When we no longer spend energy maintaining appearances, we discover a deeper steadiness beneath.

What makes authenticity vulnerable is also what gives it power. To live openly risks misunderstanding, yet it opens the door to genuine belonging. To speak truth risks disapproval, yet it establishes self-trust. To be seen risks rejection, yet it frees us from hiding. Authenticity may not promise comfort, but it offers wholeness.

As authenticity takes root, it subtly reshapes the space around us. Our willingness to be real invites others to soften their own defenses. Presence becomes permission. Without instruction, we signal that honesty is safe, that wholeness is possible, that freedom begins with truth.

Authenticity naturally seeks its next expression. For living true inwardly is one step; allowing that truth to shape our words, relationships, and choices is another. This is where authenticity becomes honesty.

Liberation Through Honesty

Honesty is more than a virtue; it is a liberating force. It releases us from the invisible labor of maintaining what is untrue. When honesty is absent, life divides: inner knowing is hidden behind outward presentation. This division is costly. It erodes peace and scatters energy.

When honesty becomes our way of being, coherence returns. What we speak aligns with what we know. What we offer outward reflects what we carry inward. This congruence is freedom—not because life becomes simpler, but because we are no longer split.

Honesty is not bluntness. It is truth shaped by care. It respects timing, relationship, and context. Sometimes honesty speaks; sometimes it listens. Sometimes it names; sometimes it waits. Its power lies not in imposition, but in presence. Truth offered with compassion becomes an invitation rather than a demand.

The most transformative honesty is often self-directed. It is the willingness to admit when we are depleted, even if expectations persist. To acknowledge when a situation no longer nourishes us, even if it appears stable. To tell ourselves what we truly desire, even when it disrupts familiar patterns. This honesty may unsettle, but it also restores integrity. Once truth is acknowledged, self-betrayal loses its invisibility.

Living honestly does not eliminate discomfort. It may shift dynamics or invite misunderstanding. Yet what it offers is profound: inner spaciousness, self-trust, and the deep relief of no longer pretending. We stop gripping control because we are no longer guarding a façade.

Honesty also ripples outward. It clarifies connection. It creates room for intimacy. Others sense when nothing essential is being withheld. In this transparency, relationship finds ground.

The release honesty offers is not the absence of fear, but the presence of truth. It is the courage to live undivided. And from this place, something else unfolds naturally: a life lived honestly becomes a gift.

Living as Gift to Self and World

When we live truthfully, the effects extend beyond us. The freedom that self-honoring cultivates and honesty stabilizes begins to move outward. A life lived in integrity becomes both an act of self-respect and an offering to the world.

To live as a gift to ourselves is to treat our lives as worthy of care. It is to respond to need without judgment, to honor rest as wisdom, to recognize limits as intelligence rather than inadequacy. This is not indulgence; it is reverence. When we tend ourselves with respect, our presence steadies and our capacity to meet life expands.

What is cultivated inwardly expresses itself outwardly. A person at ease with themselves carries a steady trustworthiness. Others sense that performance is unnecessary in their presence. Without announcement, such a life offers permission: you may be real here.

Living as a gift does not require spectacle. It appears in attention, listening, and sincerity. In joy expressed freely. In grief allowed without concealment. In faithfulness to ordinary acts of care. Presence itself becomes the offering.

Each of us carries a distinct note in the harmony of being. When lived, it enriches the whole. When suppressed, something essential is muted. Living honestly allows that note to sound — not loudly, but clearly.

Self-honoring and community are not opposites. They are mutually sustaining. The more we root ourselves in truth, the more generously we can meet others. The more we honor our own life, the more naturally we recognize the sacredness of all life.

To live as a gift is not to overextend, but to be real. It is to offer what is true rather than what is expected. And that, in itself, is enough.

Closing Reflection

Freedom through self-honoring is steady and enduring. It does not declare completion. It unfolds as a continual return to truth and a gentle refusal to abandon oneself. Authenticity draws us out from behind adaptation. Honesty gives that truth form. Living as a gift is their natural expression.

This freedom does not require perfection. It invites presence. It allows us to speak without disguise, to rest without justification, to trust ourselves without needing proof. Wholeness here is not something achieved, but something inhabited.

This freedom is never solitary. When we honor ourselves, others feel it. Presence becomes permission. Integrity becomes offering. Without effort, a life lived in truth blesses the larger whole.

Here the spiral widens again. Self-honoring does not end the journey; it deepens it. Seeking, finding, and being reveal themselves as movements of one living rhythm—not destinations, but ways of belonging.

This is the freedom that has been waiting all along: not the freedom to become someone else, but the freedom to finally live as who we are.

Not a finish line, but a return.
Not a task, but a way of seeing.
To seek, to find, and to be.

Chapter 15

Seek. Find. Be.

The soul does not seek to arrive, but to live.
— *Kea Rivers*

E very soul carries within it a rhythm—quiet, steady, persistent—that shapes the journey of becoming. It is the rhythm of seeking, the rhythm of finding, the rhythm of being. These are not three separate paths, nor rigid stages of progress. They are movements of the same dance, currents of the same river, pulses of the same heartbeat. We live them not once, but again and again, each time circling deeper into truth.

Seeking is the stirring of aliveness. It arises when achievements lose their shine, when comforts no longer satisfy, when silence begins to ask questions we cannot dismiss. To seek is to honor the soul's inner motion—its refusal to settle for surface living. Seeking does not mean we are lost; it means we are awake. It means something within us recognizes that there is more.

Finding is the quiet astonishment of recognition—the discovery that the treasure we longed for was never absent, only unnoticed. It is the unveiling of presence, the mirror of life reflecting us back to ourselves, the gentle joy of realizing that what we once pursued outwardly has always lived within. To find is to remember—to recover what has been waiting

161

patiently all along.

Being is the embodiment of that remembering. It is not merely knowing, but living—allowing truth to shape thought, word, and deed; moving in resonance rather than control; honoring ourselves and offering our lives as gift. Being does not end seeking, nor does it eliminate longing. Instead, it infuses seeking with presence and carries longing with openness. Being is the soul's quiet affirmation: you are home already—now live from here.

Seeking, finding, and being are not steps on a straight path. They are woven together in a living spiral, each containing the others. Seeking already holds the seed of finding, for the stirring itself is evidence of life awakening within. Finding naturally deepens into being, for each glimpse of inner truth roots us more firmly in presence. Being, in turn, becomes a new kind of seeking, for the soul is infinite—always inviting us toward greater depth, love, and wholeness.

This spiral frees us from the illusion of perfection. Perfection imagines a finish line—a flawless end-state where nothing more is required. But life does not unfold that way. It moves through rhythms of forgetting and remembering, wandering and returning, longing and fulfillment. Each cycle is not a misstep, but a deepening. Forgetting makes remembering more spacious. Wandering ripens wisdom that a straight path could never offer.

Longing keeps the heart open to what is beyond the familiar, while fulfillment reminds us that what we seek has always been near. The journey is not a ladder to climb, but a current to move with. The invitation is not to arrive once and for all, but to awaken again and again—to trust the turning, to honor the rhythm, and to live within the unfolding movement of becoming.

Seek. Find. Be.

These are not instructions.
They are invitations.
They are not commands.
They are reminders.
They are not a path to somewhere else—
they are the pulse of what is already within you.

The journey was never been about becoming someone new.
It has always been about remembering who you already are—
and daring to live from that truth.

Seen this way, a deeper recognition opens: creation is not something you do, but something you are. Long before you shaped outcomes or offered gifts to the world, you were already creation embodied—a living expression of life unfolding into form. Your presence creates. Your awareness shapes. Your way of being ripples outward, touching more than you may ever see.

When creation is understood as identity rather than

performance, the weight of effortful proving begins to fall away. Worth is no longer measured by output or approval. Meaning is no longer something to earn. Your very existence becomes the offering. A kind word shifts the atmosphere. A pause invites peace. An honest breath alters the field. Creation moves through you not because you strain to make it happen, but because you allow it.

To live this way is to live in trust—trust that life knows how to express itself through you, trust that resonance will guide you into the right forms at the right time, trust that even when the impact is unseen, your being is shaping the world. You are not an isolated spark, but a living note in a vast harmony, a thread in an infinite tapestry. Without your note, something essential would be missing.

This is the culmination of the journey—and its continuation.
Seeking awakened the hunger.
Finding revealed the treasure.
Being embodied the truth.

And now the spiral carries you here: to the knowing that creation itself is your nature, and the way you live is the art.

The invitation that remains is simple and profound:
live as creator.

Not by proving your worth, but by embodying it.
Not by performing for recognition, but by aligning with truth.

Not by waiting for permission, but by trusting the life moving through you.

The spiral will continue.
The stirring will return, and you will seek.
New recognitions will emerge, and you will find.
Presence will deepen, and you will be.

Each turn will carry you not farther away, but deeper in.
Each cycle will return you to the same truth—
held with greater capacity.

This is not a finish line.
It is a way of living.

Seek.
Find.
Be.

And live as creator.

The journey does not end—it deepens.

When we recognize creation as our nature, authenticity follows, and the human journey becomes a sacred expression of Spirit.
— Kea Rivers

Closing Author Note

The path of seeking, finding, and being can sometimes feel solitary, for no one else can walk into the depths of your soul. Yet this solitude is not abandonment. Beneath it, there is a presence that does not leave—Spirit with you, breath by breath. And though your steps are uniquely yours, you are never walking alone. Others, too, are tracing their spirals of becoming.

This book was never meant to give answers, but to offer invitations. Not steps to follow, but seeds—reminders to trust your own path.

In *Becoming Who You Already Are*, I shared reflections from my journey of remembering. In *Returning to Myself*, I offered echoes that taught me self-acceptance and harmony with deeper truth. Here, in *Seek. Find. Be.*, the focus turns fully toward you—and the sacred gift of creation that belongs to each of us.

If these words have stirred something within you, then the journey is already alive. May it keep unfolding in rhythms only your soul knows.

Thank you for letting me walk beside you for a time.

With gratitude,
Kea Rivers

Benediction

Seek, and you will hear the whisper that was always yours.
Find, and you will touch the treasure hidden in plain sight.
Be, and you will discover you are already whole.

This is the rhythm of the soul—not a task to complete, but a dance to live. Seeking does not end when we find, and finding does not end when we begin to be. Each movement flows into the next, circling and spiraling, deepening and widening, always bringing us back to what has been within us from the beginning.

You may forget. You may wander. You may return again and again. This is not a departure from the truth—it is the way of the living soul. Wholeness is not a destination, but a motion: a continual remembering of what has never been lost.

The truth of who you are does not need to be achieved. It longs only to be lived. Each breath is a chance to return. Each choice is a chance to create. Each moment is a chance to honor the Divine presence that breathes through you.

As you leave these pages, may you walk not as one carrying a new expectation, but as one awakened to a deeper freedom. May your seeking remain alive, your finding be tender, and your being radiant with the quiet strength of presence.

And above all, may you live as the creator you have always been—shaping, unfolding, and becoming, not by effort alone, but by the sacred truth of your own being.

About the Author

Kea Rivers is a contemplative writer, spiritual seeker, and sacred truth-teller who honors the path of inner becoming as both mystery and remembrance.

In *Seek. Find. Be: Know Thyself as Conscious Creator*, she offers reflections on the living rhythm of seeking, finding, and being —not as fixed answers, but as invitations to discover what creation looks like uniquely for each soul. Her words are meant to plant seeds rather than provide conclusions, inviting readers into a deeper recognition of the truth that has always been present within.

Her work affirms that the journey of knowing oneself is not linear, but a spiral of hunger, discovery, and embodiment. She writes not to direct, but to accompany—creating space for readers to explore what being means to them beyond inherited patterns and external conditioning.

WORKS BY THE AUTHOR:

The Know Thyself Series
- *Becoming Who You Already Are: A Journey of Self-Discovery and Spiritual Remembering* (Book One)
- *Returning to Myself: A Soulful Path to Self-Acceptance* (Book Two)
- *Seek. Find. Be.: Know Thyself as Conscious Creator* (Book Three)

About the Author

Other Works

- *Mirror Mirror: A New Vision of the Soul (Revised & Expanded Edition)*
- *Mirror Mirror: Seeing Past the Reflection (Original Edition)*